Bias Was a Genius

The Diversity Practitioners Handbook

Bias Was a Genius

The Diversity Practitioners Handbook

A Guide to Meaningful Integration of
Diversity and Inclusion in Business Strategy
and Personal Approaches

Tim Hardy-Lenik

BUSINESS
BOOKS

Winchester, UK
Washington, USA

JOHN HUNT PUBLISHING

First published by Business Books, 2024
Business Books is an imprint of John Hunt Publishing Ltd., No. 3 East St., Alresford,
Hampshire SO24 9EE, UK
office@jhpbooks.com
www.johnhuntpublishing.com
www.johnhuntpublishing.com/business-books

For distributor details and how to order please visit the 'Ordering' section on our website.

Text copyright: Tim Hardy-Lenik 2023

ISBN: 978 1 80341 562 8
978 1 80341 588 8 (ebook)
Library of Congress Control Number: 2023938468

A CIP catalogue record for this book is available from the British Library.

Design: Lapiz Digital Services

UK: Printed and bound by CPI Group (UK) Ltd, Croydon, CR0 4YY
Printed in North America by CPI GPS partners

We operate a distinctive and ethical publishing philosophy in
all areas of our business, from our global network of authors to
production and worldwide distribution.

Tim is a rare example of a DEI practitioner in that he has lived with the challenges of exclusion of vulnerable minorities. His guidebook provides a practical toolkit based on personal experiences of how he overcame the corporate barriers he has faced and can be used by all as a mirror of your performance against what is expected and acceptable.

The bottom-line benefits of identifying and eliminating pain points are explored as the basis for DEI interventions. This is key to engaging senior management, because investment without a forecast of return through added value and increased profitability will always be resisted.

Ian Beckett

You will hopefully learn some new concepts, see some graphics, and hear some experiences — I would be delighted if you would mention or credit where you sourced this information, however it is used.

D H-L
To my son Dylan
Whose beautiful soul
I have found no rival to eclipse
May your joy truly be ever flowing
Your learning journey be ever challenging
and your impact match the kindness of your intent

Contents

Preface

This is a short handbook written to explain how to commercialise and sustain DEI (Diversity, Equity and Inclusion) into a transformational business function beyond activism.

The biggest challenge to the DEI Agenda is that it so rarely works in partnership with the Corporate Agenda, but that's odd right? Because we know that DEI is the differentiating factor to create a high-performance culture and improve customer experience, and ultimately, business sustainability and market share.

The book is divided into three sections, which represent the three key Greek Delphic tenants, written by Bias of Priene (see what I did there!). Did that title make you pick it up? Didn't get what you were thinking in a book about unconscious bias? Good, I'm here to disrupt your thinking.

Section one (know thyself): explores the as-is state (our why). It discusses the challenges to DEI as well as the reasons we engage in the practice as businesses and practitioners.

Section two (certainty brings trouble): explores the essential DEI **theories** required to be analysed, understood and interpreted in a business context at a variety of levels, to ensure that any activity is built through an integrity of approach, alignment to the corporate aims and a sustainable future. It also explores the **strategic competencies** to execute DEI, how to communicate it, and manage the run-rates, reporting and activity across a global or matrixed organisation so that the impact matches the intent set out in the theory.

Section three (nothing to excess): explores the competencies of the DEI practitioner to generate and sustain change, and acts as a cautionary reminder of reactive activism versus commercial interests.

We finish the handbook naming the most pressing issues with a call to action for practitioners, changemakers and allies.

Foreword

DEI is at a crossroads. The shock of watching the 8-minute video of George Floyd being brutally murdered by the institution that was supposed to keep him safe has gradually worn off. In places like the US and the UK, your position on DEI increasingly puts you at odds with some friends, family members, and co-workers. As a long-time, ardent supporter of DEI, I fear we're losing our way. The conversations surrounding DEI seem to be creating more divides rather than driving inclusion.

DEI practitioners are rightfully frustrated that too little real change is happening. Many are shouting at white, straight guys to wake the hell up and quit perpetuating patriarchal white supremacy. At the same time, many executives have shifted from asking me, "How can we do better?" to whispering in my ear, "I give up. No matter what I do, it's never enough. We've invested a lot in DEI but we're going to quietly pull away."

Just about the time I'm about to lose hope, along comes this book from my friend and colleague Tim Hardy-Lenik. Tim shares his first-hand experience with abuse, discrimination, and marginalization. But what you're about to read is more than Tim's story. They have provided us with an insightful guide on how to do DEI better.

I love the way Tim weaves together his personal journey with his expertise as one of the top DEI leaders in the UK. They provoke us to think about strategic issues like the pros and cons of regulation, how to successfully measure DEI, the links to ESG (Environment, Social and Governance), the critical skills needed to support all people, and so much more. Reading this feels a lot like when I sit down with Tim to share a Gin n' Tonic. He's disarming, invitational, provocative, challenging, and deeply practical all in the same conversation.

I'm confident that you will not only gain enormous guidance from *Bias was a Genius* but you'll be inspired. Tim's life and work give me hope that we can move forward, rather than backward, in working together to build a more culturally intelligent world where everyone belongs and thrives.

David Livermore, PhD

Acknowledgements

With my thanks to my wonderful peers and friends at the Society of Leadership Fellows, to David and Ian for their wisdom and challenge. Thanks to Dad for his thought partnership. Thanks to Minaxi, Christina and Ritika for championing me and for your unrelenting encouragement.

Abbreviations or Acronyms

DEI – Diversity Equity and Inclusion

ESG – Environment, Social, Governance

EVP – Employee Value Proposition

SDGs – Sustainable Development Goals

UN – United Nations

POSH – Prevention of Sexual Harassment (India)

EEO – Equal Employment Opportunity (US)

LGBTQIA+ – Umbrella Term for the LGBT+ Community

KPI – Key Performance Indicator

GRI – Global Reporting Initiative

SASB – Sustainability Accounting Standards Board

TCFD – Taskforce on Climate-related Financial Disclosures

Introduction

How many times have you seen a company who stated their unwavering support for diversity and inclusion do something which shows complete apathy and indifference to inclusion?

This begs the question, how on earth are companies making these decisions given the huge wave of new Diversity, Equity and Inclusion practitioners (DEI practitioners) which have been hired in the last few years? Well, not only are we are often outside the tent pissing in, but more often than not, many DEI practitioners are under the tent getting pissed on.

But why is that, when so many businesses have shared their public commitments to diversity and inclusion? Were the companies disingenuous in their approach? Were the roles which they hired set-up for success? Do we understand the skills needed to affect change as DEI practitioners? Do we know how to make meaningful change?

I suggest it is likely a combination of all the above and much more. Now, I don't want to get into the blame game of this company said that, but they're doing this; fundamentally I think people want to do the right thing. Essentially DEI as a practice is hugely misunderstood, even by many DEI practitioners, so is it any wonder we are struggling to shift the dial across multiple companies, countries and industries?

This book provides an overview of some of the key challenges to DEI, and some tried and tested solutions to get diversity and inclusion onto the agenda in a sustainable and meaningful way.

After requests and prompts from my peers to share some of my thoughts on how to address some of the major challenges to DEI, I am doing just that in this short book.

I know how quickly our understanding and perception changes and develops in this space, and it is my hope that the knowledge and perspective I offer here will quickly become a common way of thinking and will also be challenged with another perspective. I hope that in years to come I read this back with a treasure trove of new learning and approaches to challenge and elevate this thinking. In other words, don't take my word for it. Balance my perspective with someone else's, and whose perspective is better than your own? I hope you can take whatever is most useful to you from this book and also enjoy some of my dry wit throughout.

SECTION 1:

KNOW THYSELF – THE WHY OF DEI

How many times have you heard the words 'the business case for diversity' in the last six-months? Are you heartily sick of hearing that? Well... let's take a moment and examine that feeling.

In this section we will explore the reason why we do this work, share some of my own story why, and explore the main challenges facing the DEI profession today, which compounds the 'why' as an immediate priority for us to address.

You and I know that actively advocating for diversity and designing for inclusion is morally right, and for many of us why we do what we do. Often, we start this work where we can improve the experience of other marginalised groups and seek to address social injustices because of moments in our own lived experiences and pasts which we have felt compelled to rectify. Of the DEI practitioners I know, there are a great many who have a beautiful story; where trauma and pain from their past has become a passion to improve the experience of others and make better the environment in which they were wronged. To put it simply, we enter this work as activists, but is that sustainable in a commercial context?

We will discuss a little more about the drive of individuals, indeed, we will explore some of my own drive and story behind my journey into this space; because knowing the driving force behind an individual working in this space, better helps us understand who they are, where they are coming from, and what they may be intending.

As practitioners we are completely bought-in to the concept of inclusion, diversity, belonging, equity — you name it we want it! So, it can be a bit jarring when companies and reports talk about the business case for diversity and inclusion.

Chapter 1.
The Why of DEI – For Business

As practitioners we have historically focused on changing people's hearts and minds, rather than their approach and actions; that's one reason why so many of us care deeply about the language of intent as to why businesses engage in DEI activity. There is a strong emotional connection to the work.

Another reason why so many of us find that the concept of a business case for diversity leaves a metallic and rather sour taste in the mouth is because business needs as the *sole* driver for DEI is a dangerous concept. What if it stops making business sense? Will we stop doing DEI? The good news is that study after study proves that a diverse workforce equates to better financial returns, or that a more inclusive environment results in better engagement, retention and lower hiring costs, so there is little danger of the psychology of global workforces and people engagement changing drastically enough to alter this concept.

However, the narrative of the business case can suggest to some, that profit, operating margins or annual objectives always take precedence over the work of diversity and inclusion. That is a dangerous concept.

Now I am going to say something which may be contentious — I don't believe diversity and inclusion should always be the daily executive priority in a business.

Wait, stop, before you put this book down and use it as the new coaster for your desk coffee, hear me out! If diversity and inclusion is always a priority in the business then we are not integrating our work effectively and are not catching the issues we need to consider before they go to the executive level for consideration. DEI always being at the top of the agenda is not realistic to modern business operations and fuels a cycle of reactionary behaviour driven by leadership.

Diversity and inclusion should be integrated into all parts of the business, not be a stand-alone function delivering training here and policy reviews there. Done well, diversity and inclusion thought processes are present in all stages of business decision making, and that way it becomes a daily action rather than a daily executive priority.

There is still a lot of work to do to help businesses understand the link between profitability and inclusion. Many businesses need help to understand that diversity and inclusion has a direct correlation to the commercial success of their business, through a variety of avenues, ranging from retention and acquisition of talent, and innovation from an internal culture perspective. Still, many more businesses require support and often use expensive tools and consultancies to understand how diversity and inclusion can benefit their product or services and give them a competitive market edge in their sector or niche.

There are two why's of DEI: the business case and the moral case. We have spoken a bit about the business case and how, when integrated effectively, there are returns to be gained from innovation and engagement. But what about the moral case?

Well, morality is relative, so let's anchor it to something. Let's start with the UN Declaration of Human Rights:

Article 1: All human beings are born free and equal in dignity and rights. They are endowed with reason and conscience and should act towards one another in a spirit of brotherhood.

Article 7: All are equal before the law and are entitled without any discrimination to equal protection of the law. All are entitled to equal protection against any discrimination in violation of this Declaration and against any incitement to such discrimination.[1]

Pretty solid as a universal declaration (although the reference to the 'brotherhood'; was written in 1948, and there is better and less gendered language we can use these days). So, if we take the concept of human dignity, equality and acting towards one another in a familial way, we have some core internationally agreed concepts to get behind.

Latterly, the successor to the UN Millennium Goals are the new UN Sustainable Development Goals (SDGs); these seventeen globally agreed goals go into greater detail about a whole host of aims which the international community want to see our world community achieve, and yes, equality is in there. So, we can say that the moral case for diversity, built off the back of the UN Declaration of Human Rights is still going strong.

Goal 3 - Good Health and Wellbeing;
Goal 5 - Gender Equality;

---

1 Universal Declaration of Human Rights (1948), United Nations. United Nations. Available at: https://www.un.org/en/about-us/universal-declaration-of-human-rights

Goal 10 - Reduced Inequalities;
Goal 16 - Peace, Justice and strong institutions[2]

Ok so we have a moral case for equality I hear you say; what about inclusion, and what about equity? If the global community were one business, operating in one culture, maybe our goals would speak more to inclusion, equity and historic injustices. But the language of the international community has to meet the needs of the majority of its members and so the language is a little behind where we are aiming for as DEI practitioners.

Yes, we want to talk about equity, rebalancing those historic injustices and institutional inequities which have led to socio-economic issues, entrenched racism and pinkwashing to name but a few issues. I am not suggesting that the statements put out from the international community are the basis or source for our collective moral reasons 'why'; I am demonstrating that there is a global start to the conversation, and... yes, it has only just started. We as practitioners need to keep reminding the communities we serve the reasons this is important and build on the concepts of equality.

Now, the moral and business cases are both perfectly valid. The moral case centres the individuals, and the business case centres the organisation. When we are talking about sustainable and meaningful diversity and inclusion change programmes within the context of a business, made up of individuals, we need to apply both these concepts to our reasons.

The only question you as a reader, a practitioner or a changemaker need to answer is; are you driven more by morality or business needs? We'll get onto how to answer that question a little later on.

---

2 The 17 goals of sustainable development (2015), United Nations. United Nations. Available at: https://sdgs.un.org/goals

Chapter 2.
Know Thyself – My Why of DEI

ΓΝΩΘΙ ΣΑΥΤΟΝ
gnōthi seautón

It is said that the above lettering used to be carved into the entrance of the Temple of Apollo in Delphi, all those thousands of years ago. The man who is often held responsible for these words, and many other wise sayings (also known as the *Delphic Maxims*) was known by the name of Bias of Priene, one of the Seven Sages of Ancient Greece.

Bias was a genius. He knew the path to wisdom and meaningful, effective change started from knowledge of self. He posited three fundamental truths which I believe can be applied throughout our personal and business lives to this day.

Knowledge of self, self-regulation, and finding the balance between 'doing' versus 'being' is a particular challenge for practitioners working in the DEI space, and that is why to me, the man named Bias, was a genius.

Now I should also say that even geniuses aren't people who get everything right; there are parts of Bias's works that charge up my inspiration-batteries, and others where my eyes are rolling out-loud. For example, I disagree with Bias when he says 'most men are bad'. Maybe he was having a bad day when he wrote that; possibly his cappuccino had too much froth and he was irate at his Ancient Greek barista, who knows! The point is, like any other person, he was inspirational, and genius, but also only had part of the story and some of his misconceptions — as well as his great ideas — made it to paper.

I believe, so deeply, that as individuals and as a society, we can spend so much time trying to find knowledge that we forget how to structure wisdom. So much of the wisdom which exists, is in abundance all around us, and the perfect example of that are these three Greek Maxims. These basic, three tenants of wisdom have been around for the best part of a thousand years, and it's for that reason I draw particular attention to them, and they form the three sections of this book:

1. **Know thyself** (the background and your why).
2. **Certainty brings trouble** (re-constructing DEI theory and strategy).
3. **Nothing to excess** (how we as individuals approach the work).

As practitioners, we are so quick to execute our strategies and action interventions that the historic wisdom, which exists all around us, can go unnoticed, and unappreciated. That is why this book pays a reference to such hidden, and sometimes overlooked areas and words of wisdom.

In this book, I'm not going to get into the historical battle over Bias's rights and wrongs and relative morality, but I am going to carefully pick the quotations which he is held accountable for, as a tool and device to drive home my points. There was a bucket-load of wisdom and self-reflection back when the Ancient Greeks were building their temples and libraries those thousands of years ago and that ancient wisdom is as relevant today as it was then.

So, whilst the business concepts in this book might change and the relevance may wane in significance, if Bias of Priene's sagely advice and aphorisms have lasted until today, maybe some of the thoughts built around those concepts of self-knowledge, and the perils of certainty and excess which we touch on in this book will have some enduring relevance in years to come.

The ancient Greek saying 'know thyself' is just the first of the three sayings which Bias is often credited for creating. This wisdom of self-knowledge and reflection is a recurring motif throughout the following years of philosophy, art and... yes, business. Knowledge of the experiences which have shaped you and why you responded to them the way you did is an important tool for every DEI practitioner to have.

Later on, in this book we will explore some practices which you as a practitioner can adopt to keep up this constant practice of self-reflection.

***

My Why

To understand your personal motivation to engage, disengage and re-engage in this transformational work is a key to unlocking self-awareness, where you can be more effective at crafting a more impactful and sustainable approach.

My reason for engaging in this work is born out of my personal experience. Each of us has a patchwork of joy and trauma in our lives, and for me, the trauma and the rather tragic story of my formative years have become the launchpad from which I took off in my approach to bring diversity and inclusion sustainability and creativity to areas which need it most.

The inequalities I experienced in my early years, and failings of institutions to protect me, was as a result of various biases, all with good intent.

My purpose is to help people to change behaviours, practices and processes, so that inequality reduces with each life we touch. My mission is to bring sustainability to the practice of diversity, equity and inclusion. Simply put, my 'why' has never changed, but my 'how' is now about proving the commercial criticality of DEI so that the change connected to my 'why' outlasts this generation and makes it unaffordable for businesses not to do the right thing.

The understanding of my own why has taken a long time. Knowledge of myself, my traumas, my drivers, and why I react, or think the way I do, is all part of why I do this work paid and unpaid, inside the workplace and in the community. To help you understand a bit more about my why, I welcome you into my story now — not to share in misery or pity, but to prove to you how we are all deeper than surface looks suggest. There is a beautiful hope, impact and change available to each of us in our stories, and how we channel the response to our experiences, whether in the moment or years later, can end up being your superpower, or your 'why'.

Trigger warning:
Let me start my story with a warning that this is a section to skip if you are triggered by eating disorders, conversion-therapy, violence, sexual assault or suicide.

If you look at me some days, you will see what looks to be a relatively atypical white British man. You might pass me in the aisle in Lidl and not give me a second glance (unless you like to window shop what's in my trolley and how much of the middle of Lidl I've raided... I do that too don't worry).

There may be other days where you look back and double take; 'why is that man wearing lipstick', 'why is his son in a dress', 'why is he parking in a disabled space'. Some of these are questions I know people have in their head, because these are questions I have overheard, or had directed to me.

I am a product of the response to my experiences. Who I am and what I choose to do is a direct result of the decisions I have made to respond to the highs and lows in my life, and in particular how I have chosen to respond to trauma. The trauma, violence and discrimination which I have encountered is what gives me my purpose and fuels my 'why'. I'll give you a brief overview of that story now.

I grew up in a strict Christian household, with loving parents who did all they could to protect and support my sister and me. They were devout and rigorous evangelists who believed in the power of family and the laws of the church. I remember from an early age, growing up hearing from my family that Santa wasn't real (in case I got him confused with Jesus), Pokémon were demons (so had to be banned at school) and Gay people were sick (and should be cured).

These are not the views of my family now; they have gone on a long and deeply personal journey for themselves, and I couldn't be prouder of the learning and unlearning they have done to accept and include within their new understanding. I stress to add, that now, they are advocates, empaths and they lead with love — but like all of us they went on a journey. But, needless to say, back in my childhood I was more than a bit confused about right and wrong or fantasy and reality.

The slow and painful perception I had as I was growing up was that my faith, family and sexuality were not compatible. I remember going to church, Sunday school and other youth events run by the community in an effort to find someone to talk to, and 'cure me' from my gayness.

I remember people praying over me, to release the demons inside me that led to this gay aberration of feelings, and devout friends I had turning their backs on me and never speaking to me again. No surprise, none of the 'cures' for my gayness worked... imagine that! So, I found myself drawn to a leader who was respected in the community, a senior pastor who I could confide in, and over the years he and I became close. This is where the next authority figure in my life betrayed me.

I won't go into too much detail here, but it's a story as old as time; young vulnerable person seeks support, older person in authority takes advantage, emotionally and sexually — we'll leave it there.

The mental anguish I had been feeling deepened over this time, and the control I needed over my environment began to manifest in suicidal attempts and eating disorders.

Over a significant period of time, the grip that the aforementioned authority figure had on my life began to falter; he was no longer the custodian of my temporal or spiritual existence. I knew something was wrong in his approach. I had found a way, outside of the support which I had been seeking, to reconcile a God of Love and my place within the Christian faith, without needing to justify myself or change my faith. I saw a simple, powerful film which showed how a devout religious mother went on a journey following the suicide of her Gay son to understand how being Gay and Christian were actually compatible (the film was *Prayers for Bobby*, a must watch and a film that honestly changed my life). This is where I started to appreciate the power of representation.

The need for this man who I had gone to for support, to 'save me and heal me' was lessened, because I could start to see how wrong he was. I confided in a friend who I met at my first Pride march what was going on, and immediately she took me to the police station, to report what was happening.

However, this is when the institution set-up to keep me safe, failed me. Upon disclosing to the police at the front desk that I was a minor and there was a person who was abusing me, I was told to leave the police station; they didn't take any details. To this day I don't understand why, and I began to feel after that interaction that I was mistaken and perhaps I wasn't in danger if the police gave me that reaction.

During this time, I started to go out on my own, and explore who I was in the context of a gay person who also had faith. I was loud, proud, colourful and wearing sequins you could spot a mile off (some things haven't changed). Back then, it may be fair to say, there was (in some places) less tolerance and more fear over LGBTQIA+ people, and I will always recall the times (yes multiple times) when I was chased by gangs of men, with bricks thrown at my head, or my body being stamped to the ground as they screamed slurs at me.

I remember on one occasion running to a policeman who I saw, and asking for help; they told me to leave the area and offered no more support. I had had enough. I was appalled at the notion of having to quite literally be told by a policeman to leave the area, without them doing anything to address the gang running towards me; in other words... run for your life.

I lodged complaints about this and other interactions with the various authorities, but these complaints were lost, and when I raised a complaint about my complaint being lost it was apparently too late to do anything about it. My attempt to get control of the situation was weighed down in red tape and administrative errors, resulting in a feeling of total powerlessness and lack of personal value. That's when I realised that I needed to start looking out for myself and stop relying on others to keep me safe.

However, the way I started looking out for myself was not me gaining control, as I thought at the time; but is when I lost control completely. The control I had been exerting over my physical body through my eating intensified. I decided I had control over what I ate and how I looked, and so developed an eating disorder, Anorexia and Bulimia Nervosa.

I remember the special juices and flavours I would make to keep myself from feeling hungry. I remember hiding food under floorboards, in cupboards and in the garden. I remember what it felt like to come back from the gym, feeling exhausted, and collapsing on the run back due to lack of energy. There was a strange euphoria found in knowing that my body was at its limit at the time, paradoxically affirming that I felt in control. If my body was to shut down, it would be on my terms.

I remember taking the bus back from school and waking up in my friend's house. I had no idea how I got there, I had passed out from lack of food, my shirt was off and my bones were sticking out, and there were tears in his mother's eyes. As I woke, I remember feeling nothing. Looking back I would have thought embarrassment or panic would have been at the forefront of my mind, but instead, my capacity for emotions were inhibited and starved.

I had managed to hide my condition for a long time, I was a master at hiding things after all, my parents and family had no idea about my sexuality, and I didn't spend enough time with them for them to figure out the control I was taking with my own body, or the other secrets I was terrified of them uncovering.

That is when I was forced into hospital. I remember the doctors examining me, and I recall the conversations about eating disorders and how it was considered a girl's disease, so perhaps I was experiencing some growth challenges in my puberty. I remember one man pointing at a leaflet for eating disorders which displayed a cartoon of a woman and asking 'is this you'. This is where I now recognise bias played a big part in my medical diagnosis, and rather glibly I now refer to this interaction as a time where a leaflet had the power to ruin my life through gender bias.

Fast forward two months I remember hearing the alarms beeping as my heart rate dropped and waking up hours later to concerned faces. At that time, I was given a week to live. And my overwhelming emotion was one of pure elation; I thought 'good, it's over' and bizarrely, 'I won'.

After this, there was a time in my life of which I have no memory, followed by about a decade of which I have very transient and sketchy memories, because my body was too weak to store and file the memories, and my brain, in trauma mode would not allow me to make new ones.

There was a huge blank space in between that diagnosis and realising some weeks later I was still in the land of the living. I wasn't happy, or sad about it, but disappointed that my body couldn't even carry out the simple act of finally stopping. The frustration I had at making it through that week (to this day I don't know how… some kind of miracle), speaks to the mental state I was in. This mental trauma and physical poor health were the perfect storm for my own mental health crisis. I recall the emotions more clearly than the events to this day.

I was in constant care for my eating disorder, where I was poked prodded, weighed and measured every day. My food intake was strictly monitored and my exercise curtailed. I perceived that there was a beauty at that time in the act of self-flagellatory anorexia, whereby I could slowly slip-away and control how I did so. I recall my reaction to the deaths of fellow patients at the time, first with jealousy, then with loneliness and a longing to be with them again, whether that was to have a companion in this life, or join then in whatever might be beyond this existence.

It was an extremely long road to recovery. A very long one. I cannot tell you how thick my NHS file is, but I'm sure it would take a few hours to burn all the way through on a log-burner. The cognitive therapies, nutritionists and even a 'citizen's arrest' from my dad, to stop me going out jogging, when I was eventually allowed home to recover.

My dad became my full time carer. I was removed from education and spent the next few years either lying in my hospital bed or at my parents' house. In this time, there was an enquiry from the police about the man who I had first reported, years ago. Someone else had disclosed a similar scenario to the authorities, and their account had been taken seriously. "Not mine. Why not mine?"

As I was a minor at the time, my parents quickly became involved and this revelation, combined with their full time care was a potentially explosive situation. But it didn't ignite. Instead, they were there to support my physical health so totally and uncompromisingly and lovingly that it became impossible for my mental health not to improve alongside it. It was in this time where I came-out to my father, who's initial reaction was unexpected. I won't write in this book what he said to me, that's between him and I, but what I will say, is that regardless of the potential security of my soul, his priority was my safety in the present, and making sure I knew I was loved.

I didn't have that moment of catharsis with my own mother until I heard she had directed her Church to politely 'do one' and told them to stick their opinion of me as a gay person somewhere where the sun didn't shine. An unexpected reaction, and when I asked them both, they said they were more scared of losing me than fearful of what I am. Fear can make monsters of some, but it can make lonely martyrs and loving mothers out of others.

After years of feeling unloved, unnecessary and irrelevant, I finally felt seen and appreciated. Though there is no magic wand to cure a mental health condition, especially not one with a grip as tight as Anorexia, who I called 'my friend Ana'. Among my many hospital appointments, I was one day given some news, which shouldn't have been shocking, but it was.

My mind had started to heal, it didn't want to die, and had hope. I found out that my self-inflicted starvation had cost me greatly; the tests they had run had shown that my body was shutting down, I had trauma to all my major organs, and long-term diagnosis of osteoporosis and other medical conditions; Ana had eaten away not just my mind, but my body too. That is when I had the fight in me enough to make a change. I started to realise that Ana was an enemy, and the institutions and individuals who had wronged me, were themselves wrong, and needed to be changed. And if not by me, by who?

Was I a model 12, 13 or 15 year old? Ha-ha.... no. I was more than a bit off the rails, hanging around in places I shouldn't have been, and doing things which I was far too young to do. My stomach was pumped for alcohol poisoning more times than I would care to remember. The feeling of overwhelming anxiety at not knowing where I was or how I got there was alarming. As a vulnerable individual who needed spiritual, physical and emotional affirmation, I found that I was repeatedly trapped in a cycle of situations where I was the victim of a pattern of abuse from individuals who I had (in retrospect, clearly) sought out to protect me. I remember a period of my life where I chose to sleep on the streets, and I would weep as I fell asleep, cold and lonely, and bizarrely this was a revelation. I appeared to be a younger white man on hard times, and I had people come up to me and offer money to me to get a bed for the night. But my

Black friends and older friends in the same situation or stretch of road couldn't have been treated with more indifference. This is where I started to see a real pattern of how privilege plays out in every situation; even sleeping on the streets I had privilege.

I returned to part time education part way through the year and studied hard to stay on top of the curriculum, so I had a chance of going to university one day, to learn the skills I needed to effect the changes that were needed so that fewer people had to experience what I had ever again. Of course, I still needed to be in hospital, GPs, physio, dieticians, therapy — oh you name it, I had an appointment for it! So, I had to miss a great deal of my college/Sixth Form education, and a month before the exams I was asked to leave due to 'my commitment'. I made a mental note there of another organisation and institution to add to my list who needed some education in how to support people in crisis, rather than tearing down people trying who were trying to build themselves up, for the sake of the optics of a grade average. Another institution didn't allow their one size fits all approach to support me.

So, with a month to go before the exams, I learned an entirely new curriculum, and, well, actually by conventional standards I performed pretty poorly. But those are the results I am proudest of. I might not have achieved a D or even a C, but context reigns supreme over all our life experiences (and this is another reason why if I see a job advert with the 'BA 2:1 requirement or above' I run as fast as I can in the opposite direction away from that company).

Part of my assessment for this new curriculum was in English Language Studies, and I was tasked by a compassionate teacher to write about my experience with Ana in my coursework, as poetry, and so, at 15 years old, I wrote my own version of anti-anorexia propaganda. When I need help in choosing to stay estranged from Ana, I read what I wrote all those years ago, and remember that I am worth so much more than the ignorance, opinions and cruelty which can be displayed by others to me.

Anorexia is something you never really, truly, deeply recover from, well, anyway I can't. It is something as deep rooted as a mindset to come back to, and how can you recover from a mindset, when mindsets can shift so swiftly. Anorexia is a mask I choose no longer to wear, and the story doesn't end there. I could take up many more pages talking about how previous colleagues and leaders I have worked with have treated my disabilities as inconveniences and subsequently exposed me to hostile behaviour; I could talk about a justice system and courts which could be seen not to be weighted towards the victims, and I could talk about the injustice and inequities of trying to start a same-sex family, living as a genderqueer person, a single father or a person with a hidden disability. I will let the tale end there but I have given you an understanding of why I have the fire I do.

My purpose is derived from my formative experiences, and I use that purpose to bring empathy context, and understanding into people's lives. It stems from a place of feeling wronged by institutions and people. These institutions had biases, or conscious will to act as they did, which meant that the one-size fits all approaches allowed me to slip through every net of support. That's how it was to me — a male-presenting, white, home-county-accented, younger person. And that's when I asked: If I had it that bad, what was it like for other people who didn't have the same privileges I had?

The traumas and trials we all go through in life are not ranked by some cosmic scorecard over who had it worse or better. Rather, to each of us, the things we have experienced are unique to us, and how we respond shapes us and informs who we are. My own experiences shaped my need for justice, education and equity. I also recognise that being able to write about this is a privilege in and of itself. In addition to my appearance as a white (male-presenting) person, I had a family who could support me, I survived and got a taste of justice. Many others didn't and haven't got any justice; the institutions still have approaches where some people fall through the gaps and don't get the support they need in crisis. That is my 'why'.

Chapter 3.
Key Challenges Facing DEI

In this chapter I will detail the key challenges facing the DEI profession, and we will explore them in some detail.

There are so many challenges facing the concept and industry of diversity, equity and inclusion. With some saying the global DEI industry is projected to exceed over £11 billion by 2026, there is rightly a set of questions being asked about return on investment to the businesses, sustainability of the industry and most importantly (depending on your perspective) the impact to groups of individuals who are from underrepresented groups.

Now, I'm not suggesting that this book is going to hand out resolutions to a global industry which is worth billions or identify particular organisations which may fall short of, or lead meaningful DEI activity. Instead, I am going to offer my own solutions to these challenges in Section 2 of this book to issues which are too often part of the DEI agenda from my experience.

The key challenges facing DEI are:

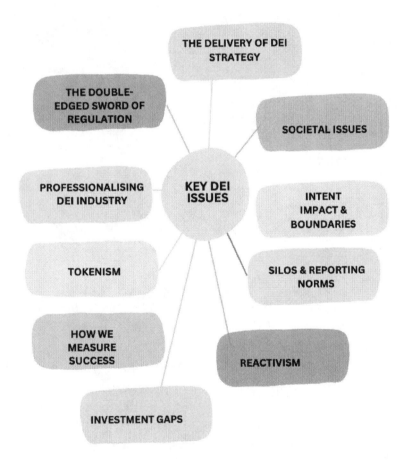

3.1 The double-edged sword of regulation

The first of the key challenges facing DEI is regulation. 'If we don't do this quickly then we expose ourselves to a potential litigious or reputational risk.' How many times have you heard something like that being used as an opening salvo in a conversation about the timing and topic of a conversation and ambition related to DEI or ESG (Environmental, Social and Governance)?

Mandatory Regulation

The relatively recent rise in regulatory standards, ranging from the legally required Gender Pay Gap disclosures in the UK, through to the POSH practices in India and EEO rules in the US, have forced organisations to ensure that an element of DEI is on their agenda. But herein lies a problem — this is not DEI — this is reporting.

The disclosure of data and adherence to legislature cannot be conflated with meaningful DEI activity, which is by definition about disruption. Your organisation's legally enforceable duties are not part of the DEI work, but merely one of the ever growing metrics through which to track your social impact credentials.

The good news is, this could be working, albeit it slowly; the Gender Pay Gap in the UK came into force in 2017, and in the last five years the number of women in FTSE350 board roles has increased by nearly half. But as anyone who has a background in data and analytics will tell you: data lies, and like an artist with a brush, data can be made to paint a picture which is partly true and skew the facts to present a rose-tinted reality.

Let's use an example, imagine I have an executive team of twelve people, and of these twelve individuals, nine are male and three are female. In percentages that equates to male executives being 75 per cent and female executives are 25 per cent.

Now imagine two of my male executives are retiring, and, being a savvy CEO looking to save some expenditure, I will give existing executives the accountabilities of the two executives who are leaving my company and not backfill the roles, thereby reducing the headcount from twelve to ten.

This then brings the new percentages to 66.6 per cent male executives and 33.3 per cent female executives. With a stroke of my pen I could increase the representation of women by 8 per cent just by choosing not to backfill two roles. I haven't hired or promoted any women into my executive team. This isn't a result of a thoughtful pipeline coming to fruition. This isn't a material change in representation. But the percentages show a great improvement. You see, data lies.

Representation is part of the challenge when it comes to female representation, of course we need more women in more senior roles; and perhaps the Gender Pay Gap has played a part in helping senior leaders be mindful about gender representation when hiring at board level. Representation is one of many issues to improve, and mechanisms like the Gender Pay Gap cannot be hailed as a success until we see meaningful and substantial change, for instance in pay-parity across genders.

Data on its own is therefore meaningless unless we have analysed it, understood the root causes, have a plan to address these root causes and communicate it to all relevant stakeholders. Simply returning the data back to the government or the regulator misses the intention of the regulation, which is to drive internal equity.

The motivation to engage in regulatory activity surrounding diversity rulings is predominately driven by risk mitigation and avoidance of falling foul of brand risk or litigious challenges from the laws and rules in certain countries. Motivation to engage in DEI activity for the avoidance of business risk, can lead to an overly academic and siloed approach to the concepts of DEI.

The work can become an analytical, legal and reporting duty. The numbers can be manipulated, as we saw in the example where we reduced the headcount, and progress can be celebrated on topics where no intentional progress has been made.

Voluntary Regulation

Whereas the motivation to engage in voluntary regulation is driven more through opportunity, voluntary regulation in its more formal setting includes those ESG standards, ranging from GRI, SASB, EcoVadis and many more, which analyse broad elements of the ESG activity, including the social impact internally (DEI) and what the business does for societies externally.

These reports and rankings are a great way for businesses to demonstrate to potential investors their market viability and sustainability in a time where sustainability reporting within an ESG context is an increasing investor requirement and a growing regulatory trend, which can become a brand device unless we are careful.

The voluntary disclosures within ESG reporting often require evidence of Kpis, charters, inclusion activity, testimonials from employees and items which simple data uploads like a Gender Pay Gap wouldn't have capacity or remit to analyse. This therefore requires an intentional resource to create these assets, and for many companies this has been the catalyst to creating so many new roles within DEI.

Voluntary Benchmarking

Have you seen a neat logo in the bottom section of recruitment section for that company you want to work for? Something along the lines of 'Best Inclusive Place 2020' or 'Champion of Equality 2023'? Well, there is a place for voluntary benchmarking, but there is a danger too.

Voluntary benchmarking can serve two purposes:

1. It can serve as a valuable tool for organisations to meaningfully understand the challenges it faces specific to their organisation, through participating in a process which often requires external review and feedback.

2. Voluntary benchmarking can also be used as a tool to add value to your Employee Value Proposition (EVP), or in other words, a medal to add to your recruitment site to show people you scored well on a test about your culture. I am not going to pass judgement and preside over which

benchmarks are meaningful in their deep assessment of DEI impact and which aren't.

However, my purpose in this section is to demonstrate that the participation in some benchmarks and voluntary disclosure activity can be driven from a desire to add to the ESG narrative or EVP credentials, rather than to meaningfully understand the issues and opportunities relevant to improving DEI in your business.

Depending on the motivation of an organisation these voluntary benchmarks can do more harm to DEI than good; if an organisation enters a benchmark and has expert writers who gild the true reality of DEI within the organisation, then there are misaligned expectations of inclusion for existing and potential employees which may also have implications for retention, and employee buy-in to the corporate culture, hindering any longer term DEI efforts.

3.2 How we measure success

The first of the key challenges facing DEI is how we measure success. *'Congratulations you are now a diverse company'*... What? Yeah, I don't get it either, but I was in a call when those words were said to a company by a consultant many years back. The individual who issued that congratulatory remark had, in their mind, successfully delivered a transformational consultancy to make this business 'diverse'. Insert lips pursed and side-eye emoji here. I may have looked like that emoji in the room at the time too!

Can you spot the problem there? I know most of you will be rolling your eyes with a familiar understanding at this one, but, just in case you are scratching your head, let me explain.

Diversity is not a measure of success unless the diversity present is meaningfully included. Additionally, the diversity which is being spoken about here needs to be defined; was this in reference to all characteristics including LGBTQIA+ individuals, people of the Baha'i faith, and Neurodivergent employees?

No, in this case the individual was referring to women only. This claim of DEI 'success' lacked balance, precision, intention and relevance — these are key ingredients to understanding how we can measure DEI effectively; in a word — discipline.

Of the 147 Maxims (quotations) from the Seven Sages of Greece, the 21st maxim rings true and comes straight to my mind:

ΠΑΙΔΕΙΑΣ ἈΝΤΕΧΟΥ
Cling to discipline

We need to cling to our discipline, and not be distracted by what is easy, speedy or less controversial, if we choose to operate within this space and retain our professional integrity.

Balance, Precision, Intention and Relevance are the key ingredients of discipline; when these elements are in alignment and speak to the needs and the representation of the few as well as the many, then we are on the right path to match our integrity with our discipline.

Balance, Intention, Precision, Relevance

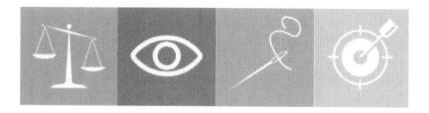

So let's explore that discipline in measuring success:

Balance

Inclusion without diversity is like a piano with no keys; it looks great but it can't play a good tune. You could have fantastic inclusion scores, they could be through the roof, but if most of your employees have overly shared characteristics (like 90 per cent of them are white, male and over 40), then 90 per cent of your inclusion scores could be expected to be good given the historic advantages and privileges associated with this group.

So, are you getting a true reading of your inclusion if you don't have diversity? No. You are likely getting a self-congratulatory pat on the back. Inclusion without diversity of representation could instead be seen as homogeneity, free from the barriers which diverse groups of people face.

Diversity without inclusion is just as problematic. Some organisations hire Diversity Recruiters and don't invest in meaningfully shifting the culture of access and inclusion for the employees who are within the company already. Representational diversity on its own doesn't shift innovation or provide diversity of thought. Actually the opposite can be true. Homogenous teams can perform more efficiently; they have a shared language and communication shortcut. However, if diverse teams are enabled with cultural intelligence to voice dissenting opinions, alternative options and perspectives free (at the very least) from repercussion, then you unlock cognitive dissonance leading to innovation and commercial success. It's the difference between diversity of workforce and diversity of thought.

The optics of representational diversity is often the first thing people seek to measure in this space; it has roots in regulatory reporting, it is quantifiable and we can affect the numbers easily. But as we saw earlier, numbers can lie.

A focus on diversity without inclusion is tokenism. This approach extracts the representational legitimacy of the underrepresented group to bolster the credentials of the business, without any meaningful intention to include them.

A good way to approach this balance is to analyse inclusion scores by representational diversity to get your scorecard of where you need to improve by region, function and demographic and celebrate any successes.

Precision

Are you a practitioner who sometimes wonders what to measure? Maybe your business is focusing on representational diversity and increasing that board level representation from 20 per cent of this to 25 per cent of that. Maybe your business wants to understand how many Black people or Women have been hired in the last year. The issue which is at the core of the precision imbalance comes from misaligned reporting expectations and organisational DEI aims between the practitioners and the leadership.

As is inevitable with any board and executive reporting, the headlines are wanted, the key numbers condensed and the figures put in a red, amber or green (RAG) format to help busy leaders understand whether DEI is on track or off track. This over-simplifies the business of DEI to boil it down to a set of numbers about representation. There are of course figures which should be standardised and reported to the executive; the question we need to answer is, are we using the right figures now?

In order to gain a precision in what KPIs are required in an effective DEI strategy we need to be data informed and insight led. What does that mean? Well, it's all very well aiming to increase hiring of women year on year, and if that's the aim and your company is succeeding then fantastic well done! But have you actually made meaningful change, or merely hit a data point?

Are these women being hired into lower paid roles? Are lower paid roles where the representational gender imbalance is? Are women staying with the company, or leaving at a faster rate than men?

By analysing the aim for an increase in the number of women being hired year on year with just some of the questions above, you can start to see that singular data aims like this are often flawed, and only take into account one small part of a bigger employee story.

An alternative way to reporting by singular data points is through data storytelling. Choosing the key employee metrics which are relevant to your business and the concepts of people management in general, you can create a snapshot in time to identify where there may be pain points in the business, or contradictions to any potentially good news stories. We can explore this in the example table below:

Headcount Leadership Team	No. of Women Leadership Team	% of Women Leadership Team	Representational % Change
Q1	96	45	46.90%	x
Q2	84	43	51.20%	4.30%

This chart shows that the representational percentage of women in leadership has increased by 4.3 per cent. Without adding in the context of the decrease in headcount this could be heralded as a great success in representational diversity. Whereas the reality is that the female headcount has reduced, but just at a slower rate than the men's headcount; this could be due to voluntary or involuntary turnover. The increase in women's percentage of representation, when viewed on its own out of context does not reflect the reality of the organisational workforce trends.

The interpretation, synthesis and repackaging of multiple data strands to provide a top-line overview to an executive, and a nuanced set of actions per country or business area takes acute analytical skill and developed maturity around the data collection processes. We as practitioners should ask ourselves whether we have this skill inbuilt into our profession at this stage. Do we accept the narrower data-led focus areas of boards and executives because we haven't defined our own version of what success looks like? Do we challenge the boards to have a more nuanced and commercially relevant aim?

The effective DEI practitioner will have aims and KPIs relevant to representational diversity, and inclusion scores for each of the demographics (from age, through to socio-economic status) across different countries, job functions and seniority levels. This often means that the burden for telling the story of the holistic DEI journey falls to DEI practitioners to be able to interpret complex sets of data.

Intention

What was the businesses' aim for this work? Were DEI roles created to be able to back-up public statements made about being inclusive? Was it to increase the number of women or underrepresented groups in leadership roles to score better on ESG ratings?

Was it to holistically examine and improve with the employee lifecycle the experiences of all people, including underrepresented groups so that creativity, innovation and productivity could flourish?

These reasons may not be mutually exclusive, but we as practitioners need to be clear what the original intention was for and our roles in the context of the business we are in at the moment.

If we don't understand how DEI got to the table, we may not end up serving the dish which is expected. If we surprise our executive sponsors in delivering something which was not the original intent, we could find our budgets cut or roles questioned. The original intent of the DEI function may have been a façade to back-up statements with no intent of follow-through. This is where the DEI practitioner should challenge the business; is that success, is that commercially viable? The good news is that ethics and commercial success are increasingly interwoven.

Ὁ μέλλεις, δός
Do what you mean to do

For DEI programmes and strategies in general, in many companies the intention now rests within the ESG narrative; being able to speak with legitimacy about the company's social impact both internal and external. The investment in this area comes with an additional element of improving employee engagement through inclusion programming which can add to the Employee Value Proposition (EVP) and be a key tool in the 'war for talent'. Though strangely, it seems that the 'war for talent' is actually being waged by companies' systems and processes against themselves. Talented candidates are everywhere, but companies get in their own way in securing them (with obvious pipeline issues in certain professions where skills are a scarcity).

We should be mindful about our intentions when we establish and operate smaller DEI sprints and projects, not just the broad motivations of the business. What are our own motivations for establishing that Employee Resource Group (ERG)?

Are we considering how this shifts the access to opportunity, or creating work and energy so that it looks good? Are the people who will lead this ERG given the tools, access and resources they need to affect any changes within its charter. Ensuring our intention matches our integrity is a key tool in helping us develop our daily discipline within this space.

Relevance

Finally, what is the relevance of any of this work? Is the work relevant to the people it aims to serve, does it know which people it hasn't served yet, and is it relevant to the areas it operates within?

'DEI is a nice small acronym with the biggest possible job; to assess, access and improve the human condition where we are needed most.'

There is so much to do, and more work needed now, than any one of us in our lifetime can achieve. This is a relatively new industry, though the core concepts of human kindness, compassion and decency are as old as time immemorial (if at times conveniently forgotten). We have to prioritise our work where it will make the most impact.

Those working to embed DEI into businesses and societies may see some returns on our work, but it will be limited against our overall personal mission. We are gardeners, planting seeds, watering them, pruning them and knowing that we will never get to experience the shade cast from branches which will grow long after we are gone. So we need to prioritise our work and make impact now so we can feel some of that inclusive shade today.

Now, if we were always going to prioritise our work where we could make the most impact, I could start my DEI strategies with a key focus on the most pressing representational and inclusion issues which could affect the needs of the many (e.g. neurodiversity and socio-economic inequalities). But is this utilitarian approach inclusive and equitable? These are issues which, if we could start to address them, would improve inclusion scores and access across multiple demographic areas, but depending on my organisation I may need to focus on particular demographics such as age or race as the areas which have the most pressing inclusion needs.

With relevance also comes pragmatism, and being able to demonstrate return on investment to the business is critical. There is more data on other demographics, some data legally required to collect, and therefore we can as a business start with the data we have most of, a very sensible and pragmatic approach. But is it always the most impactful? (e.g. the Gender Pay Gap only examines binary sex, not gender diversity).

This need to demonstrate return on investment to the business may diminish over time as more businesses understand the longer term returns within this space. As practitioners we are tasked to sustain the momentum on topics which require our attention, and we must be driven by the available data, our insight and an understanding of root causes.

Τέχνη χρῶ
Use your skill

We need to better use our analytical skills and our insight into the challenges we know local geographies are facing as their priorities. I don't know if in my lifetime there will be a company, new to the DEI space, whose first priority will be socio-economic inequalities? Maybe! In order for us to have relevance and impact we need to improve our data collection and reduce our need to justify the impact of our industry to businesses which have already invested in us.

Instead, we could use that energy to explore and gather information from qualitative research to address root causes of inequalities, where we have insufficient data to make that an organisational priority.

In the precision section, we spoke briefly about what functional areas, geographies or levels are represented in the KPIs. The need to ensure relevance of the goals and programmes to the communities you operate in is of paramount importance.

Imagine being based in Malaysia as part of a global company and being told by your Diversity Lead about global People of Colour — is ethnicity the key priority in Malaysia? Does it resonate or is it DEI enforcing cultural imperialistic KPIs? Have we as DEI Leads just demonstrated our ignorance to the needs of the Malaysian employees and further disengaged them from our own agenda.

Well-meaning aims, and global DEI strategies, are often only informed by a select number of (Western) perspectives, and often don't make regional reference to the priorities in the countries and regions they operate in.

I have lost track of the number of times I have applied to a role in the UK and being asked the standard US Diversity Questions: am I a native Hawaiian or Pacific Islander, White American etc? None of them are relevant. In my case I refuse to answer questions where the options are not compatible with my reality — others however will answer.

This lack of tailored data and aims to the countries you operate in, further compromises your global data, and thus your ability to interpret it and set a clear, informed and evidence led strategy in the long term.

3.3 Professionalising DEI industry

The third of the key challenges facing DEI is the professionalisation and expertise of the DEI practitioners.

Have you had a conversation with a DEI leader who may have 'burned out' or has said they 'didn't feel set up to succeed'? There can be many reasons behind this, but I believe a key reason why the turnover in DEI roles is so high, is because as an industry we haven't agreed on the core skills, experience, and criteria of what makes a good DEI practitioner. Without these skills agreed and defined, we can't plan out a development route for aspiring practitioners, who would be good leaders and who are good contributors, who have balanced their energy for activism with their skills in integrating DEI into the commercial viability of the business. We've all seen the incredible rise in hiring DEI leads and expanding DEI teams in the last few years. The pace of this hiring was driven by multiple angles, including burgeoning ESG reporting demands and organisations being expected to back up the public statements they made in the wake of the murder of George Floyd as two notable catalysts. The pace of the hiring and expansion of DEI roles has not happened in conjunction with a cross-industry agreement of what a good DEI skills framework looks like.

There is a debate raging in the DEI industry about what skills and competencies are pre-requisites to be effective in this space. Some people extoll the need for lived experience of inequalities as essential, and some further suggest 'anyone without lived experience of inequalities has no business being in this space' — (yes, an actual conversation I overheard). Other people suggest that DEI is, at its core, a transformative change management practice and the need to understand the academic theory of change management is the most critical aspect for a successful DEI skillset. I don't have all the answers, but I know that knowledge, experience and behaviours are key ingredients in any role to be effective.

As a profession, where many of our businesses and industries have invested heavily in our creation, we are now under the shadow of a ticking clock to create sustainable, measurable and relevant impact. Due to the fact that there isn't an agreement on what skills are required to do this work, and the dial on this topic can tangibly shift, some companies are not hiring people for these roles who are set up for success and can meaningfully effect the changes they would want to achieve. This creates an issue both for the individual and the business.

The misunderstanding of the skills required to be a DEI practitioner is one of the biggest risks to our industry. If a company invests heavily in DEI roles, and little is achieved, the company may not perceive the issue to be in their own corporate understanding of what skills are required to do the role, but rather, they may question if the concept and execution of DEI within their business warrants the investment it has received.

It is therefore beholden on us as practitioners to define, develop and agree a profession map for DEI practitioners to help businesses understand what skills are required for the aims they are hoping to achieve. I will provide my own view on how we can balance these perspectives in this section. From my experience working with, and as a DEI practitioner and leader across multiple organisations, industries and geographies, I have determined a short list of essential competencies which are required to be an impactful DEI change-maker:

Transformative change management: Delivering change through others and integrating core concepts beyond transactional approaches is a critical skill for DEI practitioners. Failure to deliver change through others traps us in a cycle of transactional projects, and siloed change, ultimately leading to limited impact and a question about the value of the function. Engaging people in this way is essential to turn strategy from a word document into action in your colleague's behaviours.

DEI subject matter expertise: Know your subject, know caselaw, know legislative trends, know the business trends and language. It is critical that we are informed practitioners. If we are not informed with the theory and current issues, we cannot hope to predict the impact of our actions or plan for future intended outcomes with realistic credibility. Would you feel comfortable leading this work in the UK if you didn't know the nine-protected characteristics of the 2010 Equality Act, or leading this work in South Africa without understanding BBBEE regulations? We need to know our craft, and this is continual education in a fast evolving space.

Self-awareness, reflection and wisdom: Know what and who influences you and how you apply your personal wisdom to your design, delivery and review of DEI. In order to be effective practitioners, we need to be beyond informed, we need to be balanced. We are often so busy 'doing' and executing plans that we rarely stop and allow ourselves to understand our personal motivation, alignment to our purpose and how we could better impact our work through careful reflection on patterns and trends around us.

Self-care and resilience: You cannot pour from an empty cup. When are you being less than your fully effective self? So many of us enter this profession in altruistic intent often with scars from encounters with discrimination and can sometimes be tasked to resolve issues which may themselves trigger us, so know how to say no, and step away when needed. We need to understand the difference between professional resilience and personal endurance; am I doing this work which needs to pull upon my skills to craft a hard-to-win change, or am I engaging in a Sisyphean task which detracts from my potential impact?

Courage and communication: This role takes guts, no doubt about it. We won't always get it right, and we likely won't always please everybody. Remember your purpose. Is it to be liked, or is it to make impact and disrupt inequities? Activism versus Integration.

The status quo won't thank us for changing it, and we are often in charged conversations with people on both sides of the conversation. We need to navigate the business needs and often the needs of the underrepresented. We may not always be able to go as far as we'd like to go, so how do we challenge that when we need to, and how do you communicate that when we can't change it.

Know how and when to speak up to power, and ensure integrity of balance between what is said and what is done.

Business savvy: Know how to use data and insight to speak the language of the business; how can DEI drive your growth, or fuel your sustainability as a business. Know how to add value to the business objectives, and how DEI can be the differentiator between the business achieving its corporate aims or operating at a better margin, through aligning DEI to the direction of the business and not the activism of the individual alone (not that personal activism isn't important!).

Empathic understanding: This space needs emotional intelligence, and patience. We will be in the room or on the call when some of the hardest to hear conversations occur and some of the poorest choices of words are used. As practitioners we need to balance the need to support and safeguard the communities who have historic and present disadvantages and inequities and also provide space for people who may behave or speak in an un-inclusive way, to feel supported to ask questions, and learn that they need to unlearn actions, words or thought processes.

In order for people to get to the learning zone which so many of our organisations will require, we need to define where our redlines are. Do we have zero tolerance on some issues and not others? If we have zero tolerance, what does that mean for how we engage well-meaning people who make mistakes. The concept of zero tolerance is dangerous, when misunderstood. Zero tolerance for violence, absolutely! Zero tolerance for language is tricky, and discourages dialogue, discourse and learning leading to growth.

One of my friends identifies as Queer, and another identifies as Gay. My friend identifying as Gay is offended by the term Queer, whereas my Queer friend sees that as an accurate identification of their identity. We need empathy and understanding of the situational contexts, emotions and lived realities of people so that we can navigate these areas with tact, diplomacy and upholding dignity. Zero tolerance in some areas can add barriers to us as practitioners to engage those who we need to shift into learning.

Hardy-Lenik: Seven competencies for DEI practitioners

As a group of DEI practitioners, we need to agree on the key competencies required to be an effective DEI professional, welcome in the newer DEI professionals and create a united approach to the sustainability of our profession. Goodwill and honest intentions do not qualify someone for a leadership position in any role, and DEI is no exception. We need as practitioners to not only agree the competencies, but the levels of competencies required for different kind of DEI leadership roles.

3.4 Tokenism

The fourth of the key challenges facing DEI sustainability and impact is tokenism.

I don't know about you, but I am exhausted with the number of times I have seen organisations consciously, and unconsciously, use communications opportunities to 'take a stand' and 'declare allyship', only for those gilded words to disappear into the mysterious ether from which the executive sponsors so mysteriously appeared when it was approaching time for the annual corporate brochure.

Let me say it more plainly. The majority of millennials, the future of your workforce, will leave your company for a more inclusive one. Studies show that inclusion is the differentiator between an engaged younger workforce, and high people-attrition.

So, the appearance of tokenism is something to avoid if you care about your brand image, time to hire costs, and sustainability of innovation. Nobody wants to appear tokenistic, do they? So why do organisations act in a tokenistic way? Let's break it down:

Well-intentioned ignorance
Misinformed arrogance
Ineffectual planning

Well-intentioned Ignorance

As just one example, we've all seen the sea of rainbows during Pride month. It comes like clockwork — because it is clockwork. The months change and with it the opportunities come for organisations to show their credentials in the LGBTQIA+ space. Maybe someone in your organisation manages to persuade a senior Executive to speak at an internal event, maybe your organisation marches in a Pride parade, maybe those pictures go on their social media and into their annual impact report. And maybe… maybe that's all that happens.

All too sadly that is usually all that happens. The desire to learn can stop when the transaction is complete. The business has taken an opportunity and a headline and extracted what it perceives to be the value of the opportunity of engaging in an event like Pride, not realising that there is so much more value left untapped for the bottom line of the organisation. How much more change would we see happen if the same energy which companies put into promoting their business profile during Pride, went into addressing institutional inequities, developing underrepresented LGBTQIA+ talent or looking at their Queer owned business supplier lists?

You see the issue isn't that organisations shouldn't be celebrating Pride, they should if their employees want to. Absolutely. But the companies should be very aware that if you slap a rainbow on your LinkedIn, you best believe that we are watching whether your words and your actions align to your celebration of your allyship, or whether you are using the trauma of millions as a marketing ploy. We. Are. Watching.

Oh, and it doesn't stop there, when opportunities for the organisation to engage in an event or conversation arise, many organisations don't stop to examine if they have credibility in the space to do so, or consider if the celebration of their allyship is premature. (Could we? Should We?) I recall events about Women's Rights where only men were talking, or about Transgender Inclusion, without any Trans people in the room. No. Just no.

Although the intention to learn is laudable, and we can all champion each other to educate ourselves, for some subjects we need to be educated by the experts of lived experience. I myself have a diversity of identity, but it doesn't make me qualified to be the only person talking about a subject I have no experience of; for example I am genderqueer and not transgender, I can speak to the challenges some Trans people face, but you would get MUCH more from speaking directly with a Trans person, and I wouldn't presume to make decisions on an initiative affecting this community without deep, meaningful consultation.

Γνοὺς πρᾶττε
Act when you know

Academic understanding (understanding) and viscerally living the experience (knowing) are not the same, so although you can, and should balance the way your employees learn so that there are practitioners in the room leading the work, don't forget; 'Nothing about us without us'.

Misinformed Arrogance

"We've done the diversity bit now"..."We don't have diversity in this part of the country". I have heard these words in a variety of forms over the years more times than I can count. Often, I hear it from senior managers and mid-level managers who are suffering from the fatigue of learning about new DEI subjects, and in these cases perhaps arrogance isn't the word. With these people the challenge is how the structure and delivery of a DEI strategy is played out and we will come on to that.

However, the other people I have heard breathe a sigh of relief when the team picture is taken, the 'role models' event is complete, 'the women's fireside chat' is concluded or when the kite marks and awards go proudly up on the website for all new employees and investors to see… are the executives. The executives and the people who are directly accountable to them have a responsibility to the business and, in some cases, DEI can be seen as a distraction from the business activity, and the fleeting organisational airtime it gets is in response to the fear that they might have about publicly declaring they don't see the value. I have never known an executive leader to state that they don't see the value, though some at the start of their understanding of DEI will talk about the value which investors will see in a glossy ESG report or annual look-back, rather than the changes which can be made by encouraging cognitive dissonance, engagement and innovation.

Ineffectual Planning

I know some wonderful practitioners in the DEI space who pour their hearts and their souls into organisations to try and meaningfully shift the dial on inclusion, but for a variety of reasons have been called-out on appearing tokenistic. Why?

Well there are three reasons:

They are fighting a losing battle with their employer: Some employers don't want to focus on all characteristics, and after years of focusing on perhaps 'Women in Leadership', employees will quite understandably question how broader inequalities are represented in the agenda, from race through to religion and beyond.

A missed opportunity to communicate shared progress: I have seen communities of disadvantaged people in organisations in, perhaps, an unhealthy conflict with one another, fighting for consistent pre-eminence on the DEI agenda, and 'what-abouting' when there is a topic not entirely related to their experience. In these instances, the DEI Strategy Lead has an opportunity to plan more effectively how they communicate their activities to avoid this perception of narrow focus or tokenism. When one institutional inequity is addressed for one community, the impact isn't just limited to that particular group of disadvantaged people, it impacts everyone.

The impact of afterthoughts versus intentional of thought: This space is so massively complex that often our passion to affect change can result in jumping at chances and opportunities where there may be a short window to make an impact (often because DEI is an afterthought) which means that because the organisation may have engaged the DEI function late in the game, the DEI leader may not have sufficient time to socialise ideas, seek feedback or consult meaningfully with people with lived experiences. This can make that practitioner appear reactive, and chip-away at the trust between practitioner and employees if that dynamic is not understood or improved.

3.5 Investment gaps

The fifth of the key challenges facing DEI is gaps in investment.

What better way to illustrate the challenge of investment differentials than by sharing with you that in the past year I have been invited to 'throw my hat into the ring' for a few DEI Leader roles, the lowest paying just £30k, the highest paying £290k... yes, that's right, about ten-times more. The gap in remuneration is eye-wateringly perplexing.

But different industries pay different rates I hear you say. These two roles were in the same industry, at the same time, with almost the same role description. Which begs the question, why don't companies meaningfully invest in the roles, and align the value remuneration?

Well one of the answers we have addressed earlier. As a group of practitioners we haven't yet fully articulated what the career-map for our profession looks like, so some companies will not know how to pitch a salary to the skills required, and yes, some will always be driven by that balance sheet and calculated efficiencies, drawing upon the goodwill of the motivation behind this work.

Let's put the salary of DEI roles to side for a moment. DEI functions are often located within the HR function, though as more organisations mature their approach to DEI, there is a growing trend that the function sits in the CEO's office or similar. So, why then is it that the DEI function seems to always be the poorer cousin of its Centre of Excellence counterparts in HR, or other CEO functions?

I suggest there are a few reasons for investment gaps and value discrepancies:

Investment expectations: DEI in general takes time to see results unless you are in jurisdictions where positive-action or positive-discrimination is both legally and ethically acceptable. The expectations for an ROI (Return on Investment) on the budget in concrete deliverable terms and quantifiable numbers can be difficult for DEI practitioners to report back when the three elements of change are quantitative, qualitative and milestones achieved.

Soft-change theory: Many of the DEI activities focus on the immediate inclusion issues which address short-term inclusion issues or just representation, rather than align the DEI activity to addressing root cause engagement which affects retention, innovation and re-work cycles. These all impact upon the bottom line and ultimately profitability or commercial success of the organisation.

As practitioners we have to do better in telling the story to our own business leaders of how DEI puts dollars and pounds into the corporate coffers, as well as being an ethically cognisant function of the organisation. If we can demonstrate the impact to the operating margin of the business and balance the need to centre humanity and empathy within our approach, we can secure greater investment to achieve our aims, and achieve our personal purpose and 'why'.

Misalignment of opportunity: There's only so much money in the budget, and sadly from what I've seen a lot of the money tends to go on the glitz of DEI; the illusion of activity rather than the deep meaningful integration and development of change opportunities. I'll give you this example: an organisation I consulted with had a small DEI budget, and roughly 20 per cent of the annual budget went on developing a partnership with a charter-mark kite-mark organisation. This was a pay-to-play organisation which gave the company the ability to put their logo on the website but didn't offer any real tangible resources, critique, feedback, benchmarking or access.

This was done in the name of improving the Employee Value Proposition for potential candidates, however when it became time to review the candidate journey and make much needed system improvements and behavioural updates to the way in which recruitment had happened, the money in the budget was spent and the experiences didn't match the image portrayed by the EVP.

When organisations are in financial difficulty, or as many say, in a period of 'expense reduction' there can often be a reaction to reduce the size of 'nice to have' functions, like DEI, which if not understood or executed properly can operate soft-change rather than business value.

Alternatively, effective and sustainable DEI functions can also receive a proportional loss of the budget when organisations mandate universal cutbacks. However, in these moments it is incumbent on the organisational leaders to assess the impact of this demand. Often DEI budgets are small, and an (arbitrary 7.5 per cent) cutback in budget will dramatically impact the ability of the DEI function to execute its aims, compared with a bigger organisational structure which may have a budget ten to twenty times larger.

In situations where cuts across the organisation are mandated, it is prescient to consider what financial savings are good optics, and what are real savings, and at what opportunity cost to the business in the longer term.

3.6 Reactivism

The sixth of the key challenges facing DEI is 'Reactivism'.

One of the first things I learned when working in the humanitarian space was to ask these questions before committing to act:

Q: What is the impact of inaction?
Q: What is the cost of my ignorance in this action?

These two questions do two simple things: it helps us assess the situation surrounding a decision, and forces us to confront the impact of our own approach or knowledge gaps. DEI is a space which quite rightly has to react to the injustices which we see in our business, and where appropriate, the injustices in our society.

It can be difficult to know where to start with DEI, which seems to cover the whole of human experience, and so we are often guided by the most pressing current need which can be right and proper. However, we should be mindful that repetitious reaction to situations without addressing the root causes may use up the energy of the organisational goodwill or interest in the DEI activity and undermine perceived integrity

This also comes in the guise of organisations wanting to do the right thing in acknowledging societal inequalities where they may affect their employees. These examples came from a good friend of mine. They shared that their DEI team spent more time with senior leadership last year assessing whether to make statements in relation to shootings in America (what they would say and how they would communicate it), than they spent on building any internal DEI learning or accountability mechanism, process or activity. This is an example of where Reactivism to external events had atrophied the DEI activity and become a socially conscious brand device rather than a transformative business-change unit.

As practitioners, we often find ourselves having to navigate where we spend our time, in between addressing the root causes of DEI inequalities within the business, the immediate pressing inclusion issues within the business and the broader societal context. We will get onto this a little later.

3.7 Silos and reporting norms
The seventh of the key challenges facing DEI is silos and reporting norms. This may be an unpopular opinion, but I don't think that the conversation about where DEI sits in the organisation should be a key debate. I see this as a distraction from the key issue: is the role set-up for success regardless of reporting line, and are leaders bought in?

In many cases I have seen friends accept roles as Chief Diversity Officers reporting into the CEO, or Heads of the DEI function move out of HR to report into the Chief Exec, only to encounter issues which were unexpected.

Now I'm not saying that DEI shouldn't be at the executive level, have a seat at the table and report into the CEO, it should. However, not right away.

To set DEI up for success the function needs to have the tools to be transformative and not transactional, and to do this it needs to be able to align effectively with the core elements of the business which are responsible for setting and propagating the culture, systems, processes and infrastructure. Many find that the DEI home sits within HR, others sit within strategy functions and others still within operations. Personally, I have found that foundational DEI in its early stages of formation and execution can operate effectively within HR as a transformative Centre of Excellence (COE) free from intense executive level scrutiny and redirection of people who are not SMEs in the early stages.

DEI should indeed have a seat at the table, it should have executive accountability, but I would encourage each practitioner reading this to question whether the timing for their own organisation to have DEI Leaders at the executive level is right, and if so, great, go do it! If not, why, and how can we get it there, or in the short term ensure it is represented by an existing executive leader.

The silos that come with DEI is often as a result of immature organisational job families, structures and change-management practices. I recently worked with an organisation who had four simultaneous wellbeing programmes, none of which were in the purview of the DEI team, all related to DEI topics such as mental health, physical disability and childcare.

The silos which existed were around long before the DEI team was created, and the DEI team were tasked to bring this scattered approach into a single clear vision whilst engaging a dispersed group of people across a global business. However, to do this, the executive understood the need to support the DEI team with a broader re-structure of roles, responsibilities and reporting norms, rather than discharge the DEI team with a shepherds-crook, a sheepdog and a hope to bring in all those siloed-sheep.

The critical lesson here is in sponsorship, regardless of where the silo exists or the reporting structure is pitched (the lines of accountability not reporting lines). But the engagement of leaders is the critical tool to use through which to unlock effective change and avoid scope-creep or rework resulting from siloed activity.

3.8 Societal issues

The eighth of the key challenges facing DEI is root cause societal issues.

We can't talk about DEI without talking about broader society a little, but I am not going to get too deep into this section because quite frankly there are so many societies to explore, norms to reference and cultures to include, and there are many other wonderful books and resources which will do that far better than me. However, the point of this section is to highlight that the effective practitioner who cares about integrating DEI into the business will recognise the most pressing societal issues within the particular region, sector or job-specialism relevant to their area, and meaningfully adjust the DEI activity to reflect that societal issue.

One such issue is the systemic attainment-gap in UK Universities between Black and White students, which (and I am not making any ugly wild assumptions here) is a result of deeply engrained systemic inequalities and racism both beyond and within the institutions.

The impact of this can be felt across multiple industries, particularly in roles requiring high-entry requirements for technically challenging roles in STEM, and compounding the challenge of STEM industries to better represent the broader societies they serve. An effective practitioner will be aware of the issues facing the pipeline of talent and how their experiences may differ when they are employed alongside you, and find opportunities to reduce this gap. In this instance, this could include redressing the high-entry requirements where appropriate, investing in bursary or scholarship programmes for under-represented groups, and much more.

3.9 Intent, impact and boundaries

The ninth of the key challenges facing DEI is the culture we create or permit as others learn — in effect, calling out or calling in.

There is a difference between (i) an intentional desire to divide, (ii) an ignorant attempt to converse, and (iii) a well-meaning conversation gone wrong.

I have heard a few times that *DEI divides us, and stops us having important conversations* in a variety of formats, and actually yes, in some cases to an extent I agree, and we can reverse that where it has stopped productive conversation and learning.

Part of the work of DEI is to instil and perpetuate inclusive behaviours and actions within employees, not to change the hearts and minds of people into one homogenous altruistic state of being with the same values and ethics. It's about advocating tolerance, respect and harmony towards a common goal.

In order to educate people, and re-educate people we need to create an environment where learning is possible, and ignorance isn't a pre-requisite for disciplinary proceedings (by employers or by social jury). We need to help people move from the 'fear' zone into the learning zone if we ever expect growth and real behavioural change.

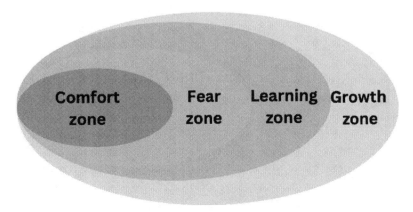

Image above shows comfort zone to growth zone journey

Let me give you an example. Two people I spent time with, both wonderful and humble souls, one an 18 year old Black man, the other a lady in her late 80s. Whilst discussing the topic of race and ethnicity the lady made a remark about 'not seeing race' to the young Black man, and in her ignorance believed that she was building a connection to this man and trying to demonstrate that she accepted him.

The intention was informed by ignorance, the impact was racism.

The young Black man explained that what she had said denied a core part of his identity, as it is clear he *is* a race, he *is* Black and that choosing not to see that contributes to the erasure of his Black identity and history. The lady was mortified and thanked the man for educating her. Both of these individuals came to talk to me about this interaction separately from one another, and both glowing about the other; one was happy to have been listened to the other happy to be educated. I haven't had many examples of these conversations going so well, where both parties were so open to sharing their truths and being open to learning, so we should ask ourselves why is this a rarity?

Learning will not always come easy, especially when our own identities are wrapped-up in the unlearning as the Ego can be a difficult beast to wrestle with. Thus being told our impact does not align with our intent can be disheartening, but shouldn't stop us from trying to learn and do better.

That's why we as practitioners need to be careful about how we interpret the themes of 'zero tolerance' to certain scenarios. We are often charged with the duty to educate and re-educate people, through *culture change*, and it is not sustainable to create a meaningful change without the safety to grow.

Ἄκουε πάντα
Listen to everyone

We should listen to everyone. Everyone has a unique perspective. What is a swear word in one culture is an expression of love in another. What is a clear red line in one culture is a grey area in another.

Now, I am not saying that all things are permissible, far from it. There have to be red lines in what a practitioner and an organisation will stand for, but I would encourage my fellow practitioners to consider, how can we shape the conversation in a way which *calls people in, not calls people out*.

I know many of you like me, will have been on the receiving end of ignorance and I freely admit I sometimes struggle to keep my cool when exposed to daily or near-daily micro-aggressions; my personal grace to let things go can be challenged. I am only human. I am not saying that we need to sacrifice our emotional radar, or that those who bear the brunt of this ignorance are charged with addressing it. I'm saying that as practitioners let's get better at making this a dialogue and not a dictate, so that people feel safe to question, query, learn and grow.

3.10 The delivery of DEI strategy

The tenth of the key challenges facing DEI is the inconsistently created and delivered DEI strategy.

There are so many expectations on DEI, to be addressing root causes of inequality, fixing immediate inclusion issues, championing enhanced access and equity initiatives, communicating about what it's doing (but not communicating too much), and engaging in appropriate communications about societal issues beyond the workplace but not appearing tokenistic.

So many DEI strategies fail because they are not appropriately designed to deliver the transformational change they aim for, and can be perceived as tokenistic or activist without substance or simply ineffectual. They play to the audience of the moment, not the problems they are there to solve.

Last year I met with a Group Head of Diversity who shared that they were at a loss to know how to balance the communication of the activity of the team with the actual activity of what the team does to the wider organisation. They shared that they had only considered behaviour change in the DEI strategy and not included systems or broader processes, and they hadn't aligned the aims of the strategy to the direction of the corporate strategy (representation and short-term engagement).

The ineffectual delivery of DEI strategies is a key challenge facing the DEI profession, which can be addressed through intentional design. In the forthcoming section I'll share some of the theory behind my model for DEI business integration (the Hardy-Lenik DEI Business Transformation Model), which helps achieve this balanced and sustainable DEI strategy by understanding the strategy behind it.

The delivery of the DEI strategy can be the undoing of many practitioners. We are tasked to keep the concepts simple and easy to understand so as to engage as many people in the change as possible. We then are rightly challenged that the concepts are not inclusive enough to represent the diaspora and intersectionality of our communities, and encouraged by our peers to demonstrate the theory of our work backed up by solid case studies, evidence and data.

In this section we outlined the key challenges facing DEI today, which explored multiple areas including:

What: (i) The delivery of the strategy; (ii) Investment gaps.

How: (i) Intent impact & boundaries; (ii) Silos & reporting norms; (iii) Reactivism; (iv) How we measure success; (v) Tokenism; (vi) Professionalising the DEI industry; (vii) Regulation.

Why: (i) Societal issues.

In the broadest terms DEI actions could be grouped into these three areas:

1. Representation
2. Immediate inclusion issues
3. Systemic root causes of inequalities/inequities

The majority of DEI strategies I have seen are great optics, but focus on representation and sometimes inclusion, but very rarely the systemic root causes of inequalities. How we structure the approach to focus upon these three areas can be further explored as we continue this exploration of how we can structure a meaningful DEI strategy in section 3, and the 60:20:20 model which outlines how a practitioner could balance these priorities to avoid tokenism, meaningfully shift the dial on inclusion and address underrepresented talent gaps.

Throughout this part of the handbook we have examined the key challenges facing DEI, and you have (hopefully) been encouraged to think about your 'why'. Why are you reading this right now? Why are you interested in this work, and what keeps you coming back? This is not a space which is easy to work in, and your purpose to enact the change must be clear to you. What will success look like, and if it is achievable for you?

SECTION 2:
CERTAINTY BRINGS TROUBLE

Ἐγγύα πάρα δ' Ἄτα
Certainty brings trouble

Chapter 1.
DEI Theory

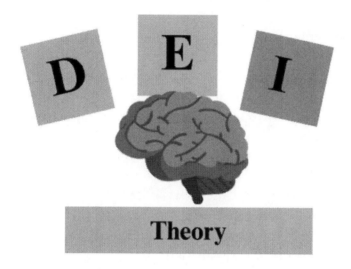

Are your senior leaders certain about the best way to engage people, include people and integrate DEI? Are you?

In this section we are going to explore the theory which DEI change agents need to examine, explore and align upon to better sustain meaningful DEI change.

The art of leading and engineering complex step change and transformation within people behaviours, organisational processes and its infrastructure requires constant reflection and tweaking to respond to the eternally evolving demands of the market. There is not one tried, tested and proven DEI change methodology which we are all following the rulebook for, but so often I have witnessed the change fall flat on its face because leaders, and yes, DEI leaders too, are unwilling to adapt their approaches, in the confidence that their own interpretation of effective change is the best version of the work. Well, let me spill the tea — you don't have it 100 per cent and neither do I, so keep tweaking and learning. Certainty in the path you've chosen can be a great thing, but a blinkered approach to developing, and tinkering with your approach to keep it healthy and relevant is required. Certainty and resoluteness can kill this work, dead, in the space of six months, and I have seen it happen time and again. Even where a DEI professional enters the organisation with the best will in the world, if they are unwilling to compromise on what they believe should be done, or the business leaders are unwilling to adopt the aims or approaches of the DEI professional, then the whole DEI function will undergo a 'restructure' and the work becomes more about the personnel management of the practitioner rather than the transformation of the business.

This entrenchment of approach can be combatted first through practitioners being cognisant of opportunity and embracing learning opportunities. Do you see the incredible importance of space, wisdom and reflection for DEI practitioners as those charged to ideate and execute this work?

Later on, we will discuss how to influence and support leaders who may have more entrenched views outside the DEI function which block the execution of the DEI activity, their reasons for doing so, and how to engage in positive cognitive dissonance, learning and challenge.

To avoid absolute statements, sweeping generalisations and unhelpful fixed metrics, we need to be able to test and validate the work of the DEI function. After all, what is diversity without inclusion, and what is inclusion without diversity?

We can measure inclusion and validate its meaning by cutting the data by demographics. The intent of inclusion, cognitive dissonance and engagement across all demographics can drive the agenda, and where appropriate, special consideration given to where there are representation gaps affecting the culture and sustainability of the organisation. This shouldn't be a game of 'who are the people?', it should be 'how do my people feel, and who are they'?

Often the answer to this can be to create a DEI strategy, and some of the key questions we need to ask ourselves as organisations and align on shared understanding can be lost when the time comes to execute change. I have found not everyone understands why, and especially to what end.

So, let's break it down, what are the core elements we would want every person working in this space to be mindful of?

When there is so much to do it can be difficult to know where to start, and the theories and structures around DEI culture change can get a little too complex when talking about effective heuristic biases and concepts which can slow us down in our understanding and disengage us from pulling the divergent strands of a coherent DEI approach together.

The coming sections outline the core components of a coherent DEI Transformation Theory Framework for DEI Business Integration, which I created in 2015 and re-worked and updated to reflect the current business trends.

The framework is intended to be structured enough that an effective DEI practitioner would be able to use it in a compelling way to validate or enhance their DEI approaches. At the same time it is fluid-enough that organisational context can be integrated into the approach.

These sections will cover multiple elements from how you can align DEI value to the business, regardless of its business trajectory, understand the business motivation across stakeholder groups and how to develop and sustain meaningful DEI change across the areas you operate in and demographics within your organisation.

We need to have the subject matter expertise and capabilities to meaningfully interrogate the results and set the standards of success and the mechanisms to achieve it. But we also need to understand change psychology and human psychology — who wants to embrace what they can't understand? We need to make the concepts of DEI accessible, and relevant to the audiences we serve.

In the next section I will outline what makes a good DEI strategy, but for now, we need to understand what the key elements of an effective DEI Business Theory are, through the aforementioned framework.

The core elements which we will cover in the next section are:

1. *Business Trajectory*
2. *DEI Motivation*
3. *Skill Maturity*
4. *Reach of impact*
5. *Perception of action*
6. *Change Philosophy*
7. *Integration maturity*

Hardy-Lenik DEI Transformation Framework
for DEI Business Integration

1.1 Business trajectory

How many times have you heard about a DEI team being reduced, or roles being cut because the business was in decline or growth had slowed? It is no secret that functions which are seen as 'nice to have' (i.e. not revenue generating) are cut first. So, the first part of the framework is to demonstrate the impact of DEI to the business and make it impossible for the business to give a dollars and pounds argument why the function must be cut, regardless of the state of the business.

To ensure DEI is of maximum value to the business, be aware of how DEI contributes to the bottom line of the business in growth or stagnation or decline.

Consider if the business revenue is significantly trending ahead or behind the expenses (running costs) of the business; this will be an indicator of the business trajectory.

In my experience, all businesses operate DEI regardless of market position as if they are in a period of growth, which does not help the function best align with the corporate agenda.

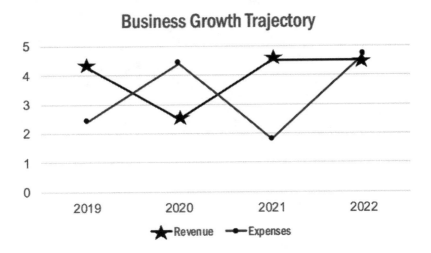

Growth: When the organisation is in a period of growth, that tends to be when DEI roles are added, to maximise on people experience and add value through creative diversity and engagement to increase the operating margin of the business or impact of the organisation.

Stagnation: When an organisation's revenue and costs are stable and their market share has remained relatively stable, the value of DEI is often not updated to reflect that fact. It has an opportunity to re-imagine the engagement of the employees, structure of systems and processes to harness the power of employee's discretionary motivation, though engagement to drive growth or a sustained business growth/ market position. To put that simply, where can DEI charge the batteries of people.

Decline (Salvage): When organisations are nosediving into the red, there is a tendency that the DEI roles are shed like a winter coat on a June day. They just can't be disposed of quickly enough. But what if, DEI functions could help organisations maximise the impact of the people resources to retain the greatest cognitive dissonance, harness innovation and avoid a total culture and skills reset and haemorrhage of critical talent; thereby retaining value in the business as long as possible.

I have seen these scenarios play-out across multiple organisations; in one case the organisation in decline got rid of their DEI team and the resulting attrition of talent (the greatest commodity of the majority of any organisations) caused the organisation to sell their business without DEI for much less than the expected price.

Alternatively, I have witnessed another organisation which was sold due to its declining profitability, where instead of the DEI function being removed from post to make room for revenue generating roles, the new owners understood the importance of DEI in reducing the feedback-time between employees and customers, the value of cultural diversity in product production and subsequent efficiencies to be made. In this example the value the DEI team could bring was vast, and the thought leadership it shared saved the company millions of dollars, through simple investigative thought practices, such as aligning people process avoiding rework and exercising cultural intelligence.

1.2 DEI motivation

Another of Bias' sayings was:

'Choose the course which you adopt with deliberation; but when you have adopted it, then persevere in it with firmness.'

DEI can blow in the wind; many organisations appear to be transient and reactionary to the work resulting from societal or organisational challenges. To pursue this work with integrity we need to ensure that our guiding-star remains steadfast and is clear to all (our mission for DEI), and that remains preserved with firmness, regardless of what changes to the execution are made along the way.

What are we trying to achieve, for ourselves, for the team, for the business, for under-represented people in the business, for society. Most companies have a clear business case as to why they undertake DEI when they are growing.

Consider the average lifespan of most companies, many slowly decline over a longer period than they grow; few if any have an eternal growth curve. Embedding DEI can maximise the engagement and increase the return to the bottom-line, and the business of business (in general) is to make money.

Consider the motivation of a business, it is rare the business objectives are purely to pursue ethical outcomes. A business to be sustainable at least requires break-even, and most require a profit to be sustainable into the future. So, let's not kid ourselves that most businesses really want us to be advocates and activists when it is not in the interest of business sustainability.

There is a lot of social impact to be made through aligning personal integrity and business purpose through the lens of DEI, if done effectively and sustainably.

Ok so let's say that the business says 'we are doing DEI to increase engagement, better our brand, avoid risk, achieve investor relations' (or all of the aforementioned). What they are saying, when you strip away the impact, is they want to improve the cash returns to the business through social engineering, and there's nothing wrong with that. But we need to make sure that we are telling that story consistently.

When we pretend that we are on an altruistic 'society-saving' mission to improve the organisation because ethics demands it of us, we do the people we seek to support a disservice. If we do this, then we pretend that our will to support their development is absolute and driven by integrity and alignment of shared values, rather than business profitability or sustainability. But yes, some companies genuinely do want to do the right thing and make money too, so how do we tell that story?

When I have taken organisations through the process in the past to examine their motivation to engage in DEI, I ask them to consider four questions. These questions are shared with the Exec Team, their Board, their DEI team and their ERGs, and the questions are:

Q1. Value: What do *you* perceive to be the value of DEI?

Q2. Positioning: How does your organisation talk about DEI in the context of these objectives?

Q3. Perspective: Do you know how to talk about the value of DEI to your different stakeholders?

Q4. Reactiveness: How do you know when to respond to a social injustice outside of the workplace?

Through the interpretation of the answers to these questions, you are able to get a cross-section view of the 'why' of DEI for key groups, tailor your communications to each group's own understanding and motivation for DEI and level-set on the business ability/intent to engage in social impact initiatives or events which are often perceived to be inextricably linked with a DEI function. Let's go into these questions in a little more detail.

Value: Consider, how does DEI support the business objectives? Is the value of DEI understood across the leadership, e.g. the role played in risk mitigation, employee engagement, R&D, and EVP?

Positioning: How does your organisation talk about DEI in the context of these objectives? If you say you are doing DEI to make money, you risk alienating the marginalised as this can appear tokenistic and can change according to the market appetite. If you state you are doing DEI for ethical reasons alone, you may lose an opportunity to reach and embed DEI into some harder to influence spaces in the organisation.

Perspective: Be clear with your DEI stakeholders and leaders about the need to prioritise the ethics of DEI as a motivator to action and be mindful about how your organisation discusses DEI across organisational communications, especially during the early stages of DEI so as to avoid virtue signalling and maximise interest.

Reactiveness: Be mindful about how your organisation reacts to world and local events which have social justice roots, and ensure any commitments or statements made can be meaningfully followed-up on, or else risk the scrutiny of the stated DEI motivation.

1.3 Change philosophy

Let's consider how we align on a change philosophy. Change in some organisations can be collaborative and in others perhaps more autocratic. Change philosophy and cultural intelligence here are inextricably linked. In high-trust environments and cultures we may find that the changes mandated by leadership are met with little resistance and executed effectively, though with perhaps a lack of connection to the visceral intent behind the changes mandated.

In high-collaboration cultures we may find that the edict from leadership to execute against a set of narrow DEI aims could actively undermine the intent of fostering an inclusive organisation which is reflective of its local cultures wherever they are located, and this is especially so within the DEI space. Often the argument for DEI is 'creative diversity' drives innovation, or as I prefer to say:

Effective cognitive dissonance from a variety of backgrounds and perspectives providing challenge and redirection. This is the difference between diversity of workforce — and diversity of thought.

Be mindful about how the philosophy of change is constructed in your organisation. The focus on ethics is often a result of leadership attempting to embed DEI without having a clear business case across multiple jurisdictions, which for global businesses can create tension where ethical norms differ.

Consider also how the philosophy of DEI can change if it rests with one or few leaders; if they leave or are replaced with less sympathetic or supportive leaders, does this risk the failed integration or rollback of DEI gains?

Consider what cultures and regions your company operates in and use the Lewis Model[3] to assess where you may benefit from a more deliberate approach to change management planning in the contexts where the change culture in place is opposed to the cultures you work within. For example, change approaches developed in a more Linear-Active culture like Denmark will not be easy for a More Reactive culture like Korea to interpret and

---

3 Lewis, R.D., *When cultures collide: Leading across cultures*. London, Boston: Nicholas Brealey Publishing (2018).

apply to its own context. To put it simply, some cultures have a tendency to follow action-chains task by task, and others use a matrixed or reactionary approach; neither is wrong, neither is right, neither is better, neither is worse. But consider how you as a leader and your business as a whole interacts with these cultures. Cultures don't stop at the country border, they are not limited to demographic groups; culture both acts as a cohesive tool within our geographies and demographics, but it also transcends our divisions and geographies. There is a different team culture between a legal professional and a marketing creative. How do you use this knowledge to its greatest effect?

Next let's consider what change we include in this approach. Fundamentally, the challenge which comes to a head in this part of the DEI integration is the mistake which so many of us have made and will likely make again:

Are we trying to change hearts and minds or are we trying to change behaviours and actions?

Much like any effective scientific experiment, an effective change programme will set out performance measures which indicate what success looks like. Early on it should be defined that the success of a DEI initiative isn't linked to the behaviour of individuals outside the workplace, but their performance is an adherence to the DEI direction and energies within their roles.

After all, to attempt to change someone's heart or mind is diametrically opposed to the concept of inclusion. As a genderqueer queer person, I know I may not be accepted fully by some individuals who may have a religious or cultural reason to object to my sexual orientation; it is no more appropriate for me to seek to change their opinion than they to change mine. However, what we must agree on in this stage is what are the 'red lines'; what behavioural respect and acceptance indicators must be upheld and perpetuated in order to foster a culture of inclusion, where there is not one super-culture judging right and wrong, but simply respects and welcomes everyone. A focus on belief change can lead to tensions and risk de-railing the DEI integration in some cases.

There is often a misconception that in order to change behaviours we need to change beliefs and values, which in my view is deeply damaging to the DEI direction. Although there may be some beliefs (say in the value of life) which we can all hold true (see UN Declaration of Human Rights), we should be extremely cautious in trying to change hearts, minds and beliefs. This can result in individuals who have different values, and often already feel marginalised, becoming further disenfranchised. If I were to work in a fictional country (Timtopia) where being Queer was not acceptable in my religion or culture, but the international corporate I worked for stated that every employee had to actively advocate for LGBTQIA+ rights, then we start to encounter change resistance and forcing a change philosophy and dogma into groups and societies which can be affected by cultural imperialism.

Now I'm not saying that organisations shouldn't advocate for equal rights, protection and safety of ALL their employees, they absolutely should. Instead, I am suggesting that the way to affect change isn't to influence someone's belief or values, but their behaviours and their actions. If I am treated with respect, and I am safe and included by the behaviours and actions of the employee who may have a cultural or moral objection to some part of my identity, then I am happy. If that person has been strong-armed into changing their perception, the reality is likely that the motivation to express prejudice continues and a hierarchy of identity begins to come into play. Some studies show that the more we deliver a view diametrically opposed with someone else's, the result isn't always learning, it is sometimes entrenchment of the original position, or that position becoming less flexible.

Instead, companies can focus on behaviour change and common behavioural expectations around trust, compassion and respect which affect the impact of the organisation, rather than influencing thinking through changing beliefs and values.

Finally let's consider the origin of the change.

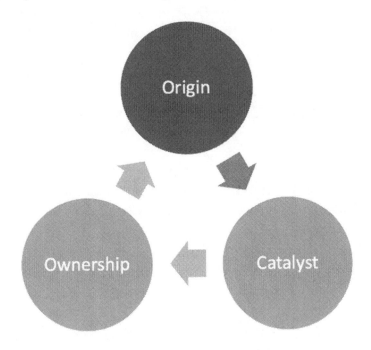

Three prompts to consider in this stage are:

Origin: Consider how DEI came into the focus at your business.

Catalyst: Was the focus following a lever event in society or the organisation which generated interest, or reaction?

Ownership: Has the work been started by a leader who has a strong vision about the 'right thing to do'?

The origin of the DEI change can impact the philosophical execution in its evolving direction. For example, I have seen organisations who have had DEI born out of the passion of individuals who I would define as change makers or activists, with a more combative approach than a coalition building approach. This method became part of the culture of DEI and the DEI leaders hired reflected the more combative edge. The DEI agenda very quickly came to be viewed as divisive, the ERGs as un-inclusive and an expensive consultant had to be bought in to redefine the approach in how the changes were executed.

That's why it's essential we understand the origin of the DEI change, the key stakeholders involved and the catalyst which has brought it to head today and the behaviours to support change philosophy.

1.4 Skill maturity

In order to make sure we are effective, we need to know how and when to partner with the business to achieve its aims, without inadvertently competing with the business.

The paradox of DEI strategies is that we need to keep DEI simple but also embrace its complexity. Be integrity backed, and projecting a welcoming, clear vision. We know that DEI is complex and needs to be backed-up by sound theory and approaches, but if we over-communicate the academic there is a disenfranchisement and loss of interest for those we are trying to reach.

We also need to ensure that there is accountability in leadership. The direction of DEI can come from the practitioners who are balancing that paradox of keeping it simple and well informed but the accountability for rewarding, scrutinising and keeping it on the agenda must sit with the top level management in the organisation for it to have meaningful integration.

Do you and your key influencers and partners understand why your organisation and smaller parts of the organisation are engaging in the DEI activity?

Some organisations engage in DEI activity to back up the performative words they have used on social media in the wake of a social justice incident. Some organisations engage in DEI to get a competitive edge, knowing that the more they do, or are seen to be doing will give them content and credibility from an ESG investor relations perspective.

Others still, embrace it as. A core part of their business identity and they know that when it is done well, it gives them a competitive edge. Take a moment and just think about why your organisation embraces DEI; ethics, profit, performance, optics, risk management? What is relevant to your business?

Often people talk about the organisation being on a journey of learning, whereas in reality that means that certain people are somewhere on the scale between unconscious incompetence and unconscious competence. Rather than every person in the organisation, it tends to be the high power or high influence groups who are on this journey to understand the 'why and the how'. For some people we rather flippantly describe DEI being in their DNA, and for others we have to design DEI in. Going with that assumption how do we find those groups of people and take them on that journey of learning?

How Can We Analyse It?

Assess: A quick way to do a light touch competence/integration check is this: imagine the hardest time in your life, and now imagine telling someone within each of these groups about that time. Are there any groups you are uncomfortable sharing this with? This may indicate that these groups don't have the empathy and compassion required as part of the CQ or EQ (Emotional or Cultural Intelligence) to build a DEI foundation and may be unconsciously incompetent in DEI concepts. One simple way I have found to analyse the competency of DEI across broad business areas is a situational question about DEI, which leaders must complete as part of an engagement (or similar) survey. This then gives insight into knowledge gaps or interest gaps. Thereafter I can use the data, cut it by region, function and other filters to understand where I need to focus my efforts in upskilling leaders across the business.

Groupings: Consider the key stakeholders, groups, teams and functions across the business. How many of these groups are unconsciously competent about DEI; and how many don't know what they don't know? Remember, we are not asking everyone to be DEI experts.

In order to do this effectively you can start by assessing the competencies of your colleagues in positional or personal power/ and influence across all fields of leadership.

Sequence: Plan which groups need to be at what level of competence to aid in the integration of DEI into the business, and by what time, to ensure that the broader DEI activity you are building can be sustained by the competencies of the business.

How can we build on the energy of those in learning mode?

Years ago, the advice I was given by a senior leader in DEI was "follow the energy of the people who support you, or you'll burn out". Whilst that advice might have been good in its time, it doesn't shift the dial meaningfully on DEI, though perhaps safeguarded my wellbeing for some time as I was in learning mode. But the intention behind those words remains sanguine; there is power and scalability in drawing upon the resources of those interested in learning, supporting and engaging in this space, so how do we do that? How can we group these actions by the four general skill competencies for additional clarity?

I suggest the below:

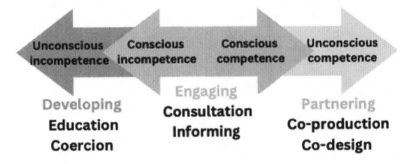

The Competency scale

How Can We Group It?

So, we have an idea of what groups to assess, but using what kind of a framework? This needs to be DEI competencies specific to your own organisation (though I will share a list of some basic competencies later), and can be grouped as below.

Unconscious incompetence: Not knowing what we don't know, and how that impacts on our business.

Conscious incompetence: Knowing we have some areas to improve and not knowing how that impacts on our business.

Conscious competence: Acting to improve and maintain certain areas of understanding, doing so purposefully across all areas.

Unconscious competence: Acting to improve and maintain certain areas of understanding, doing so as standard across all areas as part of the organisational DNA.

Individuals who are in unconscious incompetence should be afforded opportunities to develop their knowledge and understanding of the topic. In some cases access to education may not be a sufficient-enough motivator to engage these individuals and coercive power through legitimate or referent influence channels can be considered, especially after a long time where individuals have chosen to circumvent the learning opportunities made accessible to them.

Individuals who are in conscious incompetence and conscious competence are aware of their knowledge or action gaps and are actively, and consciously, putting in effort to engage in the subject. They are learning how to develop more inclusive approaches, and avoid well-meaning faux-pas or culturally insensitive remarks. These individuals, whether motivated through a desire to learn, an avoidance of embarrassment or through coercive control, are key individuals to unlock the power of your DEI activity, as so much of the DEI activity rests, unsustainably, in the in-groups and front line managers. To do this, you can consult, inform and engage this group to understand how you can better move them on through these competency stages and towards active allyship and unconscious competence.

Those in unconscious competence have put the work in; they have perhaps in some ways re-wired their thought patterns, structures or processes to make it difficult for them to do certain things which may be un-inclusive. Now, nobody is perfect and there is no such thing as a human being who lives free of the ability to cause pain, offence or make mistakes. Instead there are individuals who actively structure their environment and nurture their thought patterns to avoid mistakes — in essence, learning from the past. These individuals are often strong allies of the DEI agenda and good people to co-produce and collaborate with in a variety of partnership activities. However the risk is over-activity of partnering with this group and not nurturing the pipeline of those in the lower levels of competence. This partnership with the informed and active allies is low hanging fruit, but to shift the competency of the majority of the organisation requires deep meaningful work, to build a dispersed coalition and practice of evolving understanding as a movement, and not only a spearhead of allyship as the totality of their DEI competencies.

One example of this was an organisation I consulted with, that had a group of people (not within the DEI team) in unconscious competence and they were the de facto steering group for DEI. All activity went through this group of individuals; all learning and external events which came into the DEI team went to these individuals for their first refusal. The time and energy spent in developing these individuals into strong, informed advocates wasn't wrong. But, when asked how the people in the unconscious incompetence and conscious incompetence levels would benefit from the investment in these individuals, there was no clear answer.

Following the challenge, there was talk of how these individuals could consult with the business to develop an updated skills framework with various competency levels specifically referencing DEI, which I sincerely hope happened. However there was a missed opportunity by over-focus on one informed group, in that the majority of the organisation went un-supported. Only when challenged did the organisation see that there wasn't an alignment between the continued development of the competencies of these individuals in the

DEI leadership space and the sustainability of the DEI function, until the broader organisational employees in other levels of competence could move through the competency levels.

1.5 Reach of impact

A global strategy to include all by its very nature can sometimes do the exact opposite.

Global DEI strategies with broad aims around female representation or People of Colour may not translate to the immediate priorities and DEI landscape within local geographies. For example, in India the DEI conversation is not about People of Colour, but there is a background of religious, caste and geographic inequalities which is far more nuanced and requiring greater depth of understanding than a global 'ethnic minority' metric, given to them (often) by a centralised group function based out of a Western country. To companies who push a global approach, I say well done, but, BUT, is it locally relevant? If it isn't be prepared for your global approach to start disengaging people from your agenda.

Hopefully that shows why we need to assess the reach of DEI impact to meaningfully integrate our activity, so let's dive in. There are five areas or relevance we should consider when assessing the reach of impact:

1. Local relevance of theory
2. Personal relevance of theory
3. Demographic relevance of theory
4. Skill/ functional area relevance of theory
5. Impactful relevance of theory

Locally relevant theory: DEI strategies need to be relevant, in a variety of ways. We know that often what de-rails a DEI strategy are challenges about its legitimacy, perceived tokenism or ineffectual impact to those who need change the most. So, that means we need clarity about what are the key challenges or opportunities we need to address.

We need to make sure that relevance reigns supreme across our work. It isn't relevant to talk about People of Colour in India, or Japan when we use traditionally Western concepts of that term. Or having an organisational goal for every team to increase representation of LGBTQIA+ by 30 per cent may not be realistic if LGBTQIA+ people are already over-represented at 80 per cent representation, or you are operating in a market where there is not safety to disclose and lower benchmarks in your industry. So, are your aims relevant to all your key local areas? It's no good having a global DEI strategy if you are not applying it locally. Context is key. As always — now, and forever.

Personally relevant theory: Secondly it is critical to know how your personal purpose aligns to the change you are trying to generate. So much of our work as practitioners is motivated by our desire for social impact. We all operate within businesses, with distinct priorities, and we all operate in businesses made up of people which have different reasons for pursuing the work. As practitioners we have historically focused on changing people's hearts and minds, rather than their approach and actions; that's one reason why so many of us care deeply about the language of intent as to why businesses engage in DEI activity; there is a strong emotional connection to the work.

Demographically relevant theory: It is incredibly important that the DEI strategies reflect the hidden and overt diversity of the communities they seek to serve, and interventions or lack of action is informed through evidence and data. Additionally, we should be clear about what layers of inequality can be addressed and which are not within the current DEI approach. The five layers of inequality are:

1. Interpersonal: Behaviour between individuals
2. Internalised: Personal beliefs
3. Collective: Social norms
4. Systemic: Barriers within structures
5. Institutional: Practices which reinforce

First, we must be clear as practitioners that we understand all these layers of inequality before we start to act and then clearly articulate what layers we are addressing and why, and when, (if indeed we will), address any additional layers.

Skill/Functional Area Relevance Theory:

Finally, is your DEI strategy penetrating all the areas of the business which need it most? To use a rather clunky metaphor, are you wielding a sledgehammer or a scalpel? In instances where we wield a hammer we apply general approaches, often due to the need to simplify and call people to action,. Here we can miss an opportunity to note and address areas of particular challenge.

Let's envisage an imaginary company, let's call it Timdustries. (See what I did there...again.) Let's say that Timdustries has a great inclusion score and representation across Women, People of Colour, LGBTQIA+, and Disability, and other characteristics often tracked by ESG metrics are well above the reporting average. Does Timdustries pat itself on the back and say job well done? Well yes to some extent (with the obvious caveat that data can lie), but let's use data to go a little deeper into the pockets which need us most. Let's imagine that the majority of the representation of women came from leadership roles in business operations functions, and few were in technical or sales roles. The global message of representation and inclusion is positive by my functional area but is not as inclusive or diverse as it should be to represent the markets it operates in. That then is where the DEI energy should be directed to, rather than energy put into maintaining the status quo at a Global broad-brush level. We need to go a level deeper with our data and reporting and accountability tools to ensure total penetration of DEI into all areas of the business across functional areas.

Impactful Relevance Theory:

The anvil without the hammer is just a lump of metal... in the same way, updates to the structure and processes of the organisation without meaningful behaviour to sustain it will not create the spark which sustains change, or reinforces use of the hard-fought procedural or behavioural updates to drive organisational high-performance.

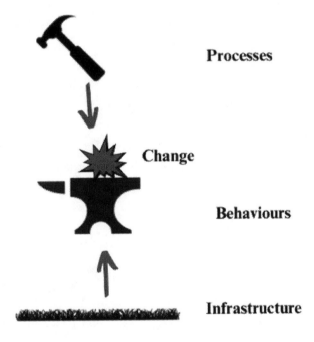

Processes

Change

Behaviours

Infrastructure

The image above shows how processes need to reinforce behaviours, and infrastructure need to support the ability to display those behaviours to create impact.

I've seen organisations quite literally spend years building and implementing a maturity matrix, only to see it crumble because the behaviours they are seeking to change are undermined and tested by the very structures and processes within the organisation.

One example which comes to mind is an organisation which worked to develop nuanced and detailed lives of what it meant to be an inclusive leader to further enhance their understanding of which mid-managers would be suitable for adding to a succession-plan for more senior internal roles. Although the behaviours were put on a beautiful sheet and the learning and development functions had done their job in bringing what that meant to life, the behaviours weren't measured in any formal way in an annual performance review. Therefore the good behaviours they were trying to shine a spotlight on were being measured against outdated and historic competencies from the old skill framework, missing an opportunity to reward the behaviours they were seeking to change.

In this way I've seen wonderful behaviour goals undone by immature process gaps, and wonderful process goals unwoven by a lack of intentional alignment with the physical and digital estate.

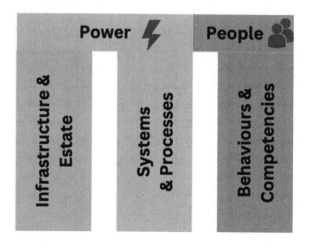

The Focus-Pillars of Transformational Cultural Change

The key foundational pillars of the scope of transformational DEI change are divided between power and people change and include systems and processes, infrastructure and estate and behaviours and competencies.

An effective practitioner will investigate and understand where there are potential synergies or blockers to the sustainability of the behaviour, process or infrastructure changes being sought as part of any DEI progress.

1.6 Perception of action

Some organisations don't communicate enough the amazing stuff they do within the DEI space, though this is the minority of organisations. Whereas other organisations over communicate what they do in the DEI space, with weekly email blasts, newsletters, and corporate messaging everywhere you look.

Why do I say over communicate? Surely the proper integration of DEI into corporate communications is a good thing? Yes. But talking at the expense of doing is so often the trend we see in this space. If you have a great story to tell about the meaningful DEI activity then by all means, communicate it, but be mindful of DEI fatigue, and be mindful of whether you are playing into a perception that your function is more talk than action.

This issue of how to balance the work of the DEI function in general is a tricky one, it navigates accusations of tokenism or lack of progress, and on the other hand a lack of collaboration, compassion or transparency.

In my experience, the majority of organisations talk about what they are going to do, and on occasion over-inflate their credentials more than they do the meaningful work to address root cause inequalities, alongside inclusion and representational issues.

This means we need to balance our action and our communication of that action. We need people to have access to DEI information to share our impact, but in order to avoid tokenism and ensure that we can meaningfully shift the dial, we need to balance this.

Some of the major issues relating to reducing engagement comes from ineffective design and execution of how DEI approaches are communicated. The continued development of DEI content, without meaningful tangible changes, creates diversity fatigue and disengagement from the change initiative.

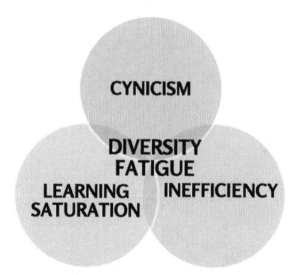

The Causes of Diversity Fatigue

Inefficient execution of DEI strategies can lead to cynicism when communication of intended action does not match the pace of communicated changes, or there is a 'saying' versus 'doing' approach which mirrors a tokenistic or shallow approach to DEI. In other cases, where organisations attempt to engage in DEI related topics by sharing content external to their organisation and beyond the scope of what they will realistically include in their DEI strategy, there is a risk that these approaches will disengage colleagues, as the cumulative impact of available learning and developments to keep up with reaches a saturation point. This can further play into the 'say versus do' gap, which ultimately leads to either cynicism or rejection of the communication of DEI subject matter.

Imagine that 60 per cent of our DEI activity focuses on addressing root cause issues and systems, processes and infrastructure (the kind of stuff people don't love to hear about, like equitable succession planning). Next, imagine that 20 per cent of the work addresses the issues for inclusion and belonging in the now which can impact people's experience. Finally imagine that 20 per cent... only 20 per cent.. condenses and crystallises the impact of that work and signposts individuals to resources. That way you can balance how you address the root cause, immediate needs and perception of action of the breadth of your strategy.

Build and execution of strategy

60% Root Causes	20% Immediate Inclusion	20% Representation
Root cause issues perpetuating inequalities		

Communication of strategy

60% Fix	20% React	20% Show
You said, we did. Alerting the business to listening conducted, systems and processes updated and equities realised.	Response to engagement and justice issues as they arise	Awareness days, fireside chats, newsletters

THL 60:20:20 model (outlining how to communicate a strategy built with integrity to focus on short medium and long term DEI actions)

Fix: This is about addressing root causes which affect long-term representation and inclusion issues. The reason this is the majority of the DEI work is because so much of the DEI activity is in the integration into all elements of the business. It requires a conscious and intentional analysis of current systems, processes, behaviours and analysing that data and insight to redesign the 'as-is' to a better 'to-be' state for the underrepresented, with an intentional focus on those root causes. When we communicate that our strategy activity is designed to support the redesign and rebalancing of equalities and equities, and this is mirrored in how we communicate our DEI activity, this speaks to the integrity behind the approach. But what about needing to respond to engagement issues we haven't planned for? This is where we react.

React: This is about inclusion and representation needs being met in the short and medium term. Many practitioners spend their time focusing on the immediate inclusion issues, which often address the soft pain points of DEI, rather than challenge the root causes leading to this inclusion issue. For example, I could spend hours developing a proposal to buy-in language translation software to address an inclusion issue with colleagues in Malaysia (outside the HQ country, UK) who feel they do not have the opportunity to develop into senior leader roles. Or, I could spend time examining the development, promotion and hiring practices of leaders beyond a certain level and why no leaders in Timdustries are based outside Europe or the UK, when over half our staff are based in South East Asia. One will put a sticking plaster on a solution, the other will address it in the long term. I am not saying there isn't a need for a sticking plaster, but we need to find practical ways to develop and sustain DEI, often with time limited resources; which would you choose?

Other examples around reaction often relate to social justice issues or crises and missed opportunities in the business relating to a particular demographic group. How we respond as a business to that can be informed by our strategy execution approaches. When I communicate my activity around how I react, we need to consider how we show we are not being tokenistic or wholly reactive — and therefore we reference how our 'Fix' approach supports this communication pillar. But what about showing we are actually moving the needle, and engaging people beyond telling them what we're doing; how do we build dialogue? This is the 'Show' pillar.

Show: This is about credibility. Say less, do more. That's the basic concept in this 60:20:20 approach. But we need to recognise that showing our work, progress or challenges is a key part of the execution of our strategy and time should be earmarked for it. Engaging people in dialogue is one way through which we can affect change, another is through making it difficult for companies (made up of people) to do the un-inclusive thing through redressing root cause inequalities. In this pillar the intent is that people who want to engage in the DEI activity can see what activity has happened at a glance, including headline activity, and have opportunities to engage in events, or join a capacity building DEI community or network. The intent of all these pillars together seek to address the challenges we so often get in DEI communication of our approaches which are:

- *You are being reactive and performative, not addressing the root causes;*
- *You haven't shown us evidence of what's changed;*
- *You haven't shown us you care about what's happening right now.*

The 60:20:20 model will help to balance meaningful action, the perception of action and the rebalancing of power dynamics to affect meaningful change. In a time where companies may be new to this work or concerned with the perception of tokenism, or ineffectual work, this model is a proven tool. It helps organisations create the structure required to create change and speak about that change with authenticity and knowledge. It also ensures that the root causes of inequality are structured to be addressed, and that there is space to tackle the immediate inclusion issues and the space to communicate the activity to drive continued engagement and learning with integrity.

***

1.7 Integration maturity

There are a variety of different ways to measure the maturity of the integration of DEI into the business. And yes there are a LOT of integration and assessment models which are behind an expensive paywall, many of which don't go nearly deep enough to understand and identify the areas they assess.

Although there is a benefit in some of the assessment tools available, and indeed there are some standards which can help businesses understand their maturity levels overall, the off-the-shelf assessment tools I have used historically and conducted by an external consultant do not have the same impact as an in-house DEI consultant using an assessment metric to review the status of maturity and integration using their own knowledge of the organisation as an internal practitioner.

Maturity Levels

In general I suggest there are five different competency levels: initiating, emerging, performing, advancing and leading.

Each of these areas has a specific approach in how they engage with DEI, and this approach may differ depending on what part of the DEI activity is being undertaken. For example, the DEI activity could be in an emergent state in the integration to talent management and in an initiating state in its approach to culture and safety. Let's go into some detail about the levels now.

The Organisational DEI Maturity Scale

1. Initiating: An approach driven by risk avoidance or legislative/contractual duty to meet regulatory expectations and respond to significant inclusion issues from employees.

2. Emerging: An approach driven by a desire to leverage DEI as a key differentiator in the EVP of the business, but the activity of the function tends to focus on immediate inclusion issues rather than root causes.

3. Performing: An approach where DEI is leveraged to add value to the overall corporate strategy but is limited in reach, though has started to address root causes issues and balance immediate inclusion issues.

4. Advancing: An approach which emphasises the value of DEI as the differentiator between business sustainability or growth, and has a focus on addressing root cause inequalities and inequities perpetuating inclusion issues.

5. Leading: An approach which centres DEI as a transformative internal practice, embedded into all areas of the business, its products, services, sustainability and external relations strategy, and addresses societal inequalities compounding organisational inequalities.

The Areas of Assessment

DEI is an ocean we could try and boil for a hundred years and we may not even fill a teacup, so we often encounter a challenge in trying to divide up and assess our impact for meaningful change. These challenges also come into play when we look at how we assess the level of our impact overall, and by the distinct areas where we can lean-into to shift the dial on inclusion by addressing root causes or immediate inclusion matters.

In the last couple of years, I have spent some time chairing the creation of the world's first cross-industry agreed benchmark to measure diversity and inclusion. As part of that process, I offered to share some of my own intellectual property, and that was how the root causes of the issues can be assessed. The issues can be graded by level of assessment using the 1-5 scale we just read about, and can be grouped into the following areas to deep dive into impact:

Hardy-Lenik DEI Integration elements

DEI Strategy: In this grouping, the maturity of the DEI strategy is assessed, ranging from what accountability mechanisms are in place, how the data and insight is collected and verified and the structure of the approach sustained across core business units.

Culture: In this grouping the reward, recognition and motivation are analysed alongside the EVP, digital and physical estate, and core policies/procedures which affect the engagement of employees.

Communication & Engagement: In this grouping the way in which DEI is communicated to the business and external stakeholders is reviewed, and the maturity of the mechanisms, groups and partnerships which may support the continued development of the function are assessed.

Talent Lifecycle: In this grouping the overall alignment to talent planning and execution is reviewed, and touches on everything from inclusive talent acquisition partnerships, through to tactical workforce planning and performance reviews, encompassing the entirety of the formal talent stages in the employee lifecycle.

Products & Services: In this grouping the way in which DEI as a function and a business competency is reflected in the products and services and serves to add value through innovation, increasing market share or maximising operational efficiencies through engagement and collaboration.

I have found that grouping the core areas of the change we are looking to build and sustain in the DEI function into the above format has helped both to identify synergies in my approach and tell the story better to internal stakeholders. It has helped me secure the resource, buy-in and support of individuals across all areas, but most especially in people leadership and executive and Board roles.

Chapter 2.
DEI Practitioners

DEI Practitioners

2.1 Deeply understanding ourselves
as DEI practitioners

We need to have clarity on our personal purpose and how it aligns to the business purpose for DEI. What is the business case for diversity.

One reason why so many of us find the concept of a business case for diversity leaves a metallic and rather sour taste in the mouth is because business needs as the *sole* driver for DEI is a dangerous concept. What if it stops making business sense? Will we stop doing DEI? The good news is that study after study proves that a diverse workforce equates to better financial returns, or that a more inclusive environment results in better engagement, retention and lower hiring costs, so there is little danger of the psychology of global workforces and people engagement changing drastically enough to alter this concept.

However, the narrative of the business case can suggest to some, that profit, operating margins or annual objectives always take precedence over the work of diversity and inclusion. That is a dangerous concept.

Now I am going to say something which may be contentious; I don't believe diversity and inclusion should always be the daily executive priority in a business.

Wait, stop, before you tune out, hear me out! If diversity and inclusion is always a priority in the business then we are not integrating our work effectively and are not catching the issues we need to consider before they go to the executive level for consideration. DEI always being at the top of the agenda is not realistic to modern business operations and fuels a cycle of reactionary behaviour driven by leadership.

Diversity and inclusion should be integrated into all parts of the business, not be a stand-alone function delivering training here and policy reviews there. Done well, diversity and inclusion thought processes are present in all stages of business decision making, and through that way it becomes a daily action (integrated) rather than a daily executive priority (reactive).

There is still a lot of work to do to help businesses understand the link between profitability and inclusion. Many businesses need help to understand that diversity and inclusion has a direct correlation to the retention and acquisition of talent and innovation from an internal culture perspective. Still, many more require support and often use expensive tools and consultancies to understand how diversity and inclusion can benefit their product or services and give them a commercial competitive market edge in their sector or niche. This is where the conversation can move more swiftly if we help leaders assessing ROI understand the link between cognitive dissonance, diversity and culture of innovation, which we explored earlier.

There are two why's of DEI, the business case and the moral case; they need to balance to work in partnership in business.

Organisational context: How many times have you come up with an amazing DEI strategy, programme or initiative and it hasn't quite had the impact you wanted?

For my part that has happened all too often, and the reason why that was the case for me, is because I didn't have enough understanding of the moving parts of the business and its priorities.

For example, I wanted to develop a women's leadership programme; the data showed through the year that satisfaction from participants were high, and women were being promoted at a higher proportional rate than before, but the representation and headcount of women in leadership wasn't shifting dramatically... why?

Well, there just weren't the roles! I hadn't aligned effectively to the future direction of the business, which was contracting in particular regions and functions and meant that fewer new roles were available. We were developing the skills and capabilities of women for leadership, but then didn't offer them promotions, so of course, that led to voluntary exits by female employees from the business as we couldn't provide the roles for women at the leadership level that they had been developed for.

The DEI ambition and the Corporate ambition were aligned, but the missing link was the understanding of the operational context of the organisation and how workforce planning of local regions or functions within the business aims impacted upon each strand of the DEI strategies.

Sustainable: Lastly, the DEI strategy needs to be measurable, repeatable and scalable. We need to be able to demonstrate the impact of our work, whatever the aims are. Some focus on representational diversity, some focus on belonging scores, some focus on both in conjunction.

However, your organisation measures success, you need to make sure you have a formula which outlasts your tenure at the organisation.

Can other people understand the way you came to the decision of what is underperforming and what is on track?

This need for strong, deep interrogative subject matter expertise leads to the paradox of DEI strategies. Build a compelling DEI theory and approach which is (likely complex) and communicate it in a simple, clear compelling way. Few people are excited by engaging in theory, execution and technical concepts, they want headlines and quick wins. Our job can be helping those headlines and quick wins speak to a long-term integrity of the work and the function.

2.2 Understanding your 'why'

This work takes a toll. It is often emotionally triggering, repetitive and can begin to feel like a Sisyphean task of trauma. I am not alone in saying that sometimes I simply run out of energy, and I need to recharge my 'why' batteries. Sometimes I do that by talking with people and hearing their stories, which charges up my 'why', which is rooted around mitigating injustices stemming from my own personal life in childhood. We each have a 'why', and it isn't always going to be a big life event, it can be a belief, conviction or a curiosity.

In the last five years, the number of DEI practitioners I have known personally to burn-out is at a percentage I believe is WELL above the average for other roles. To sustain our continued energy in this space, where frustrations can lie around corners which we weren't expecting, we need to have an emotional connection and resonance with the reason we are doing it... or at least, I do.

There may be some people out there who can see a logical reason to engage in this work and aren't flustered by setbacks and challenges along the way. However I haven't yet found those people, so my best advice is for you as a practitioner to really understand your 'why'. Why are you doing this work?

Know thyself as a concept is critical to the build and execution of DEI theory and strategy, to ensure we haven't gone off piste... or, done anything to excess. Whether that excess is in what we omit or double-click on.

Some questions I have found helpful to ask myself when I try and understand my own 'why' are:
- What am I trying to change?
- Have I done as much as I can?
- Have I done it my way, or someone else's way?
- What happens if it doesn't change?
- How do I feel about that?
- And...why?

Those who know me well will know I have a highly structured approach to most things, so my thinking and self-reflection is no exception. If this approach and structure works for you woohoo! If it isn't needed and you know your 'why' already, then let's skip forward!

2.3 Nothing to excess – commitment and work-life balance

It took me a long time to realise that I was actually part of the problem in integrating DEI effectively.

With all my good intent as a DEI Lead, and desire, passion and energy to address every inclusion issue which came in, I was failing to do two things. I was failing to make time to address the origin issues of those inclusion tensions, and because I kept all the plates spinning and few dropped and broke, I didn't let the business step up and take accountability for a broken situation, they didn't have exposure to.

In another way, my commitment to supporting people in crisis and emotional drive to connect with people was a barrier which kept me transactional and not transformational. This is so often the case I have found with DEI functions; we go in all guns blazing with the grand plan to restructure inequalities and inequities and reattribute the power dynamic bit by bit, but the reality is we get side-tracked. Often we can blame organisations for under-investing or not supporting us properly, and in many cases this is true, but we also need to take some personal accountability for what we do, and what we don't do.

If we continue to respond and react, we leave little space to plan and develop, which are much-needed practices when dismantling decades, and sometimes centuries of ingrained institutional inequities.

When I was told I wasn't being a good role model by working long hours and churning out DEI at all hours of the day, I will admit I didn't take that feedback on board at the time (and yes I really should have done). There were issues in the organisation I was working with which needed my immediate attention, otherwise I perceived the window would close, people could be emotionally hurt and the trust in the DEI function falter. I believed I just didn't have the luxury of looking like a good role model when others could be hurt.

What got me to sit up and change my behaviour was when I realised that the blocker to stopping the incident re-occurring was me. I wasn't allowing leadership to see the issues and their potential magnitude as I was managing them as they came in; firefighting. I was using all my energy with a bucket of water, waging war against an oncoming forest fire as leaders were looking the other way, and I hadn't shouted FIRE! When I understood that by adjusting where I put my energy, rather than giving all my energy, I was able to achieve a healthier work-life balance. Offsetting the emotional burden of others' trauma had to shift in my ranking of importance in order to effectively execute the work beyond a transactional approach.

We as practitioners often have a deep emotional connection to our work, and approach situations with an attitude of 'if not us then who?' Which can fuel this dependency and constant transactional state (transactionality) on us. There will always be exceptions and conversations which require us to firefight and engage and console and advocate, but we need to get that balance right and affect lasting change.

I suppose this is another way to say, working smarter, not harder, doesn't mean you sacrifice your impact in DEI; in my case it has actually unlocked my ability to bring key players along on the journey.

2.4 Impatience for change versus strategic focus of energy

We want change! When do we want it? Now.

As people with a deep resonance with the work, and a close connection to the impact of the inequalities which we are fighting against, we can often become frustrated at the pace of change.

Sometimes it seems that change is so slow it is tokenistic. Sometimes it is. Sometimes that change regresses and the hard-fought gains are back to square one, and it is depressing.

We do hear those rather glib and cliché statements about DEI being a marathon and not a sprint and catch me on the right day and I will agree with you. However, I think there is so much that could be done if our mentality and energy as a collective was focused on strategically addressing a few key shared issues; we could go far, and we could go fast.

Although I agree that substantive change from a representational perspective takes time, this notion of DEI taking a long time to achieve isn't as true for inclusion. Engagement scores increase and decrease throughout the year, and the narrative of it being a hard fought and long game to play for inclusion gains can be a damaging narrative, and a get out of jail free card to those fence-sitters of DEI or individuals who aren't wholly convinced at the value and depth it should go to. I agree meaningful inclusion takes time to nurture, and for that feeling to become a sustained pattern of inclusive behaviours; but let's remember that we can change inclusion and engagement quicker in many cases than we can change representation. So DEI is a marathon, but we need to remember where we can sprint and save our energy for doing so, rather than explaining why we can't.

2.5 Understanding of skills

This has created a tension from my perspective when it comes to the hiring of DEI practitioners.

Earlier on, we touched on the need to professionalise the DEI industry with a clear profession-map and articulation of skill competencies to do the work. In the absence of a clear guideline for aspiring DEI practitioners and leaders as well as organisations, is there any wonder that some of the criteria for the skills required has created a charged conversation in the DEI community. Loosely the conversation is divided into two areas: the first stipulating that lived experiences are a prerequisite for the ability to discharge a DEI role effectively; the other stating that transformational change abilities are the prerequisite and not lived experiences.

But what do we mean by lived experience? Are we talking about a particular lived experience? Do you have to have experience of a disability, of being gender divergent, an ethnic minority? The experiences I have had have certainly helped me in articulating my way and given me an insight into some of the root causes which perpetuate inequalities, but these experiences do not give me the skills to do anything about it. I am a DEI leader, with no lived experience of being an ethnic minority, yet I was still able to launch the charity-sector's first Anti-Racism programme and ensure through my sponsorship that this was led by a dedicated Anti-Racism leader with those lived experiences. I am not an expert of racism in my own lived experience, but I do know how to build and design a set of DEI change programmes which can have value added to them by someone who can elevate this work with their own lived experiences. No one person can hold all the identities of a diverse person, and so the concept of lived experience as a prerequisite to me is a distraction; it actually begins to police the 'why' rather than sustain the skills. So, to me the questions become:

1. *How informed is the DEI practitioner about the landscape of inequalities and inequities affecting multiple communities?*
2. *How does the DEI practitioner draw upon and defer to the knowledge, experiences and expertise of people from outside their own identity/experience groups?*

This is a sensitive conversation, and in my view our shying away from it as practitioners is playing right into the hands of those who want our practice to fail. In order to build sustainability in our function we should recognise that all lived experiences are valid to be working in this space; there is no one demographic more qualified than the other. The pre-requisite to work in this space cannot only be passion, though that is important. The prerequisites should be the same as any other business function. What are the essential criteria, and very importantly, how do you build relationships, coalitions and partnerships with all groups of people to move inclusion forward.

2.6 The practitioner and optics

Everyone is a little afraid of getting it wrong, whether that motivation comes from a genuine fear of offending, or a concern over how they are perceived, or be judged by a jury of peers or the court of public opinion. We fear being called out, and as practitioners we are held to a high standard, but these standards are not absolute. We need to extend ourselves the grace to get it wrong, and communicate our learning and growth.

You wouldn't expect a Michelin star chef to cook themselves haute cuisine every night, or a designer to only wear high fashion all day every day. There are certain roles in society where the disclosure of your role sets a target of expectation on your head.

I remember doing this first hand, to my own father. As a vicar, I had a high expectation of his behaviour and expected him to be saint-like at all times; I was waiting for the time I could say "that's not very Christian" (whatever that means). There are some roles which have authority, and these roles are the ones which we scrutinise intently.

The authority of DEI roles comes from the expectation that our behaviours should, at all times, be the template for role modelling inclusive behaviour. This can be exhausting. We are human, we make mistakes, we have gaps in our knowledge and we need to be allowed to learn with grace as well. If we as practitioners can be seen to get it wrong, this allows others to try, fail and learn.

Constantly trying to maintain this image of a practitioner without bias or knowledge gaps, can not only be exhausting but actually it can be intently damaging to our work in building knowledge and awareness of DEI concepts. When we as practitioners say "I got it wrong" it can go one of two ways: the first way is some people may use this as a reason to delegitimise our expertise; the second way is that we naturalise and normalise the process of learning. Although knowledge gaps can be seen as a weakness by some, it is important that we learn loudly and help others to feel comfortable to tell their stories about what they have uncovered in their own understanding.

2.7 Reporting

We have already touched on the challenges of how DEI impact is measured, and the need for us to tell a better story of the impact of DEI is critical to the sustainability of our function in the longer term.

The way in which investors expect change is given by rather narrow reporting metrics around representational diversity, often tied only to one market or one characteristic, that doesn't represent the impact of inclusion, but the intention towards access.

In order to tell the story of DEI better we need to understand our own impact better, and have better maturity of how we collect, interpret and forecast our data.

We can tell the story of our people engagement in relation to the level of investment we might make into development programmes, or physical estate, but for some reason we haven't cracked the code as a group of practitioners in consistently articulating the bottom line impact to the business. I suggest there are three key areas that DEI progress can be reported back against:

1. Representational
2. Experiential
3. Innovation

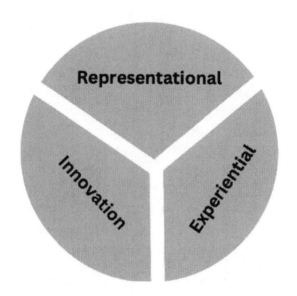

Hardy-Lenik The DEI Impact reporting wheel

Representational: This can be measured quantitatively, by the number and percentages of disclosures of a particular demographic changing over time in any particular data set from overall headcount, across levels or regions.

Experiential: This can be measured by the inclusion scores or engagement scores when cross-referenced by groups, regions and levels to understand the impact of DEI over time.

Innovation: This is a practice that DEI is attempting to instil through organisational cognitive dissonance, and so needs to nurture examples and illustrate a clear pipeline of examples where DEI behaviours have reduced the rework cycles, or time to resolve issues, or provided perspective that has altered the delivery or design of a product or service and the resulting value of that change. This needs to be a story backed by evidence.

Other practitioners have suggested that a fourth area which DEI can be measured against is 'Brand', however I would suggest that a strong brand or EVP with DEI credentials can be measured as a result of meaningful representational and experiential developments in DEI. It is possible, and indeed the norm, for organisations to develop their DEI narrative as part of their brand as aspirational targets rather than actual reflections of the current culture.

Although much of the work of DEI should be evidence based, there is a need that we supercharge our accountability of its progress and demonstrate the impact of our work beyond the data, as it can take a long time to move. In some cases this can lead to disenchanted executive sponsorship, or manipulation of the data to tell a better story than the reality. Therefore, in general there are three ways to measure the impact of the work to tell a rounded story which is to separate the DEI reporting in the aforementioned three categories into two areas.

1. What has shifted in the data

Boards and executives tend to focus on representational diversity as the measure of DEI program success. This data may be cut and digested by level, or one, perhaps two demographics and will likely include current headcount representation, hiring, promotion and retention trends; sometimes with reference to how the company is not only performing Quarter on Quarter but also compared to similar sized organisations in the same market/geography.

2. What are the milestone moments

We are all familiar with the work that it takes to establish basic structures for DEI; particularly in the creation of Employee Resource Groups. This work itself can be the result of months of hard graft engagement with colleagues and leadership, often with longer term impact which will come from the establishment of milestone moments. But their creation in themselves should also be recognised as significant in the formative stages of DEI. The recognition of what constitutes a milestone moment should be closely assessed by the DEI leader in the organisation, as there are occasions where activities or recognition may on the surface appear to be a significant step forward, but do not represent the work of meaningful integration of DEI activity. One example of this is the recognition from pay to play awards, or charter-marks, which have low thresholds for evidence and impact, but can generate a perception that the progress in DEI is beyond the actual reality of progress.

DEI Progress KPIs	Data (Long term)	Milestone (Short term)
Representational		
Experiential		
Innovation		

This graph shows how you could group the impact and KPIs you are driving forward and report that immediate progress in set-up versus material change

When we look at data as the indicator of success alone, we can sometimes become frustrated that the data doesn't reflect the value which will come from the hard work and stage-gates which have been built. So it's important we tell the story of what key activity we have been doing and how it will likely add value to the business in a simple format. One way of doing this is by following the following model.

Issue, Impact, Action Outcome

Issue: What is the problem in the business?

Impact: How will this affect ability to achieve organisational aims?

Action: What did DEI do to address this?

Outcome: What happened, or what do we expect to happen?

Here's an example of how this could be done effectively.

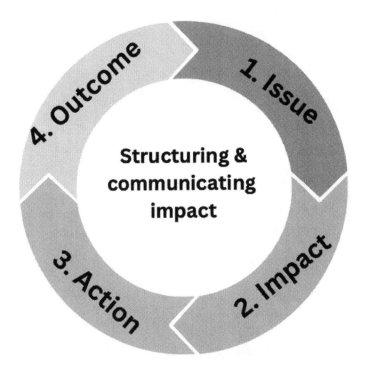

How can we deliver DEI impact and tell that story? Let's use a real life example.

Top-line Issues and Approach

Issue: Cultural intelligence in the organisation is lacking across all functional areas.

Impact: This can affect the ability to produce quality products and experiences for customers impacting the bottom line.

Action: Creation of cultural intelligence training and trial cultural collaboration initiatives.

Outcome: Increased awareness of cultural differences, and consumer and customer and colleague expectations, increasing the impact to the bottom line.

Now if we look at this as a real life example this approach can help us structure the ability to tell the story of the impact of DEI to the organisation and make the case for resource when we need to influence.

Example of a Real-Life Issue

Issue: Rejection rate of produced technology assets are high in Korean market when produced from a Filipino market.

Impact: This had a high return, distribution and brand cost affecting the profitability and operating margins of the Asian market.

Action: Awareness around consumer expectations at a different level to Filipino production, Korean-centric production and cultural context brought in to manage the production.

Outcome: Rejection rate decreased considerably resulting in higher profitability, through the use of cultural and inclusive behaviours.

Our ability to tell our stories as practitioners is something which this community is very good at as a general rule, however we need to get better at telling the story of the impact of our work on the broader business. When we do that, we can make it impossible for organisations to deny the value which DEI can bring and change it from being seen as a fluffy soft-change initiative, or a 'nice to have', and instead see it as a key lever to business sustainability or business growth.

2.8 Mindful DEI reflection

How many times have you been in panic mode with how much there is to do and started executing your activities with a frantic energy which can be matched by some of the most outlandish cartoon strips? For me, it has been many times and I would fuel a cycle of getting in my own way but I didn't know it.

During my time as a Fellow of the Society of Leadership Fellows of St George's House in Windsor Castle, I have had the honour and privilege to be challenged and nurtured in my thinking, and my approach as a leader. The barriers I couldn't name became so clear to me. To be a good leader, I need to be a wise leader.

Wise leadership means we have knowledge of self, we understand our triggers as individuals, our aims and the context of our organisation.

Knowledge of Self

I am a firm believer that we first feel things in our body before we understand them in our minds. Do you remember the butterflies in your tummy on the first day of school but didn't know how to articulate the emotion? I believe that over time we have learned to listen more to our rational mind rather than our bodily senses, which hold a great deal of wisdom. When we connect back with our senses we can enter a situation, or a decision, with the knowledge of how we feel, what is influencing us and why that is. This enables us to know whether it is the right time to make that choice and provides a spotlight on what personal biases may be affecting our approach.

Context of Our Organisations

Every organisation is different, and the situations which practitioners are in will evolve day to day, hour to hour, though I have found that much like the wisdom of the body, there is wisdom in the patterns of nature around us. One of these patterns which I structure my thinking around is the pattern of the four seasons. The seasonal approach is reminiscent of the cyclical patterns of business, as well as the cycles which happen in our personal lives. I deeply believe that there is wisdom in items, objects and elements in the world around us, such as the four seasons. There is wisdom in the seasons. We should encourage ourselves to query, what is the theme of each season, and what question does it ask us.

SPRING

WHAT NEEDS TO TAKE ROOT AND GROW?

SUMMER

WHAT NEEDS TO BE ALLOWED TO GROW WILD?

AUTUMN

WHAT NEEDS TO BE LET GO OF?

WINTER

WHAT NEEDS TO BE ENDURED?

Spring: The wisdom of spring is one of potential, where we plan and sow seeds, and think about what roots need to go deeper and whether our foundations are strengthened for the seasons to come. The question for spring is 'what needs to take root and grow'?

Summer: The wisdom for summer is one of growth and expansion, where plants are in bloom and can quickly grow wild and free, requiring little guidance or a lot of care to bring under control. The wisdom of summer is 'what are we going to allow to grow wild'?

Autumn: The wisdom of autumn is one of decline, of loss and of slowing down, where the leaves fall and growth slows. Decline and failure can be a natural part of all our journeys and sometimes we can be pushing energy to keep something alive which just isn't going to get traction. The question of autumn is 'what do we allow to be let go of'?

Winter: The wisdom of winter is one of darkness, and the absence of light is an endurance for better things to come. The question we have to sit with for the season of winter is 'what needs to be endured'. Whether that is uncertainty, mistrust, anxiety, annoyance, you name it — what is beyond our control which we need to release to be effective individuals and impactful practitioners.

Purpose Alignment

As modern workers we will have a wobbly-wobbly patchwork of jobs throughout our lives, and probably a range of industries we work in. Given that we can spend most of our waking hours in a job, we need to think carefully about what that job offers us beyond a pay cheque. How does that job align with your purpose? When I consider the job, I think about the opportunity of what I have to change, the receptivity to that change, the resources at my disposal and the agency I am given to do that work.

This begs a question we need to answer, what is my purpose? And hopefully we have somewhat answered that in understanding our 'why'. But this is a bit deeper; in this understanding of purpose it could be many things, ranging from a good work-life balance to a desire to be the first genderqueer person to lead a FTSE100 company, anything! How does your position allow you to action your purpose?

Finally, we consider, who am I as an individual? What makes me, me? Do I have to hide elements or code-switch parts of myself to fit in at work, and am I comfortable with that? Am I happier when I am doing something else? Somewhere else?

When we understand how these three elements align, Position, Purpose and Person, we are able to channel the power of our actions into a direction which helps us affirm we are in the right place, or identify barriers to achieving your purpose and activating the power of your potential.

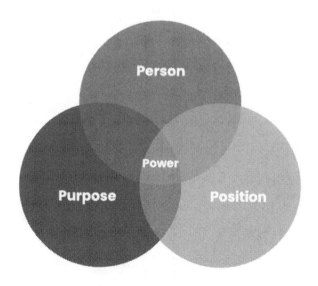

Understanding Our Aims and Timings

Effective DEI in the business context isn't activism. That took me a long time to learn how to differentiate the two.

We know that many of us engage in this activity of diversity, equity and inclusion in order to right the wrongs and injustices stemming from society and emerging in the bubbles of business. The trouble is, when we are activists in the business context we can sometimes forget to speak the language of the business. If we want to really integrate DEI into the business we have a difficult task, which is to take that passion and activism and turn it into a capability to integrate the behaviours and desire for increased DEI competencies across areas of the business, to make it difficult to ignore or do poorly or half hearted.

Coming from International Non-Governmental Organisations (INGOs) as the majority of my working background, I know how closely aligned the DEI journey can be to advocacy and campaigning for social justice, and of course there is a link, but we need to be clear about the 'what' and the 'why' of social justice for business so that the companies understand the reason they are supporting our work, for commercial gain.

The social justice work from many organisations is done through the lens of Corporate Social Responsibility (CSR) and Environment, Social Governance (ESG) reporting, and there are some truly fantastic initiatives stemming from this space which provide access and agency to underrepresented groups across global and local areas. However, there is often a conflation of that work being DEI, and although there is an element of activism in that work, we need to help organisations understand the 'why' of that work better. In order to be good global citizens and institutions, we need to re-invest our profits into the communities we profit from, or seek to employ. Although, I am painfully aware that some companies pay large sums of money into social justice the intent behind it (I have heard first-hand) has been to make that look good for the end of year report for investors, rather than strategically aligning the opportunities of where it invests to be as impactful as possible.

When organisations are intentional about where they invest social impact resources you can draw upon the energy and expertise of your DEI practitioner as an activist who will likely understand some of the societal root causes affecting the pipeline of the organisational talent. They can help direct where the resources can be most effectively positioned to not only discharge an expectation of social investment but re-funnel that energy and opportunity into future employment opportunities for groups with less access and opportunity and who may be less represented in the business.

We know that this work takes time, and we have spoken a little about pace of our work and how much we allow to fail. I am an activist who has learned how to take that hat off at work and speak business talk. Sometimes I feel like a double agent engineering social change in the wings of the organisation and pulling the strings together piece by piece to start the build of a pattern which will eventually become a tapestry depicting social justice. We have to use business to drive this; regulation and government is too slow to flex to the needs of the global community and lacks the resources.

So, let's use our time here (i) to remember what is possible in the time we have; (ii) to aim for what is not, and; (iii) build our legacy of being good ancestors to the future generation.

2.9 Understanding our triggers

Not so long ago I declined to participate in mediating and resolving an issue which was too close to my own traumas. The issue was talking about bullying, harassment and involved a disability and an eating disorder. On paper I might be one of the ideal people to bring my lived experience to that situation and enlighten some of the dialogue with my own perspective. But I knew I wasn't in the space to offer all of me, and all of my experience to resolving that situation.

My traumas are not a commodity for others, but a tool for me to use at my discretion alone.

Just because you have lived experience doesn't mean you have to give access to it, I learned the hard way that access to it is only when I am ready, and that can change day to day.

We know that there is an emotional burden on people with traumas; whether that be sexism, racism, homophobia or many of the other terrible injustices. Some of these individuals can be motivated through compassion to educate others to avoid a repeat of what occurred to them. They are beautiful souls and offer access to their experience as an opportunity for learning, and when it is offered it is such a gift. However, the emotional labour of re-educating people in DEI concepts so often falls to marginalised groups which can re-awaken traumas and experiences and compound existing inequalities.

This is exactly what happened to me, on another occasion. I was invited to speak about my experience and one of those experiences touched on homophobia. During my story I started to share details about an attack I had experienced, and as I was talking I started to shake. Unsure of what was happening, as I continued to talk I started to remember something which had clearly been pushed down and locked away for a good reason, and the act of educating others through my experience had unlocked a trauma I didn't even know was there.

In reliving the trauma, you are keeping it alive in one form, and as practitioners we can sometimes forget that our legitimacy doesn't come from our lived experience, though some of our knowledge and empathy may come from it. I learned the hard way that access to lived experience comes when I know I am ready and sharing stories must only happen when there is appropriate support for those who share them.

This is how I realised, sometimes the best person to engage in or lead the conversation isn't me, even if my experience is a direct match to the issue.

Chapter 3. DEI Strategy

DEI Strategy

3.1 Delivering a meaningful DEI strategy

DEI strategy is a cycle. So many of us have said we want to work ourselves out of a job; the reality is, we never will. Our work is cyclical, and will exist as long as business exists, inequalities exist and people are looking for a competitive edge. One way to get that is by increasing the engagement of people, increasing cognitive dissonance and making more products or services more relevant to communities and groups of people. In essence, this is about market relevance and market penetration.

DEI will likely evolve and hopefully become a function with greater traction and less urgency, as some of the societal root causes begin their long journey to being addressed. But this won't happen in my lifetime.

DEI strategies need to have a constant reassessment where they are questioned about their relevance to the key areas they seek to serve, which are the geographies of people, their identities and the business as a whole, as well as how sustainable that approach is.

Therefore, an effective DEI strategy cycle will be:

1. Sustainable
2. Locally relevant
3. Demographically relevant
4. Organisationally relevant

DEI Relevance Strategy Cycle

I have spoken about this before, but I am going to say it again, because it is so important. Global DEI strategies which fail to adopt a local nuance are doomed to appear for what they are, well intentioned shallow attempts to engage in DEI, without the resource or energy to give agency to the countries and cultures to determine their own key DEI priorities. How many times have you seen a big global organisation reporting their DEI success citing women globally (ok yes!). And People of Colour globally (sorry what?). If they are a truly global organisation, what does People of Colour mean at a global level? Are they trying to clumsily say, ethnic minorities as defined in the UK or US? Is that really a global metric or is it indicative of an immature DEI approach which conflates UK/US centricity with global relevance? You tell me.

DEI strategies which fail to be demographically relevant to the needs of their people will not be received well and will not achieve the change potential they are charged with. This is linked to geographic relevance but if we take geographic relevance away for a moment and assume that is done well, how can I, as an employer, decide what demographics are most important to add intentional energy to with my limited resources? This is where data and insight come in as your best friend. The data can justify the focus on the demographics you have chosen to give energy to, and the duty of the practitioner falls to identifying what the data doesn't disclose (for example disability disclosure is low across many businesses, but that doesn't mean it is a small issue for any business).

Organisational relevance is the alignment to business objectives, and when a DEI strategy effectively enables aspects of the organisational plans to come to fruition, it is often achieving its aims. However it should be noted that in the foundational stages of DEI, the strategy can in some cases cause friction between the existing structures and processes of how the business has been attempting to achieve its aims up until this point. The positive tension which the DEI strategy creates has to be contextualised as a positive disruptor with a longer term view of the return of this disruption.

The strategic approach has to be measurable, scalable and repeatable; so in a word, sustainable. This requires access to resource to program the change, information to evidence the focus areas and engagement solutions to demonstrate the intent and call to action of others across the business.

We outlined some of the core components of a sound DEI theory, but how do we build a solid DEI strategy? What are the core components? Don't worry, I got you!

There are a thousand-and-one different areas of the DEI strategy which we need to touch on, but let's keep it simple enough to use, and general enough to flex to the majority of organisations. To do that, I am choosing six core components of an effective DEI strategy. These components are:

1. Alignment to business direction
2. Accountability in leadership
3. Understanding the aims and reasons
4. Relevant data and insight
5. Robust decision-making framework
6. Balanced action and communication

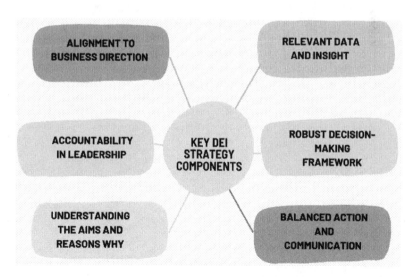

Hardy-Lenik key DEI strategy components

3.2 Alignment to business direction

Consider what the engine of your DEI strategy is, what are the top three things it will achieve in year one, and what will it do in quarter one, two, three and four respectively to stagger up to that achievement? How will these cumulative actions support the wider business trajectory and organisational mission.

By demonstrating within your strategy the alignment to the organisational priorities, as well as the operating principles you set your strategy up to be received by, internal stakeholders will offer reduced resistance as it becomes an enabling function rather than being perceived as an additional thing to do from a compliance perspective. This stage is critical to communicate effectively and harnesses the core part of the business purpose for DEI (see the earlier section of DEI Theory in Section 2, Chapter 1), and how that is reflected in the strategic deliverables.

3.3 Accountability in leadership

We hear it time and again, "DEI is so important to our business" and then leaders drop it like a stone, or don't understand how they can sustain its importance without becoming nervous of its potential impact.

An effective DEI strategy will have mechanisms in place to draw support from the executive and provide direction to the leadership on how they can meaningfully engage in the topic. In the past I have done this by developing executive action plans informed by the relevant data of a leader's organisation and assessing their engagement in three distinct areas which are:

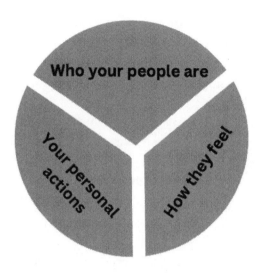

Balancing learning, engagement and representation

1. Who are the people in this leader's organisation (including demographic, levels, locations etc)?
2. How do their people feel? (Again cutting this data by all relevant demographic metrics.)
3. What has this leader done personally to develop DEI? (This reviews the learning, participation or support of the individual.)

Although we can develop complex accountability models and RACI charts, these I have found often distract from the core issue which is, leaders don't know where to start with DEI, and are under pressure from their direct reports to demonstrate what they are doing to shift DEI to tangible progress. By giving leaders the tool to say here is how 'who' (our people) have changed, and 'how they feel' has developed is an important step in bridging the accountability gap between leader and employee. In some cases, a leader may inherit an organisation with poor engagement and systemic representation issues, and in that case the third element of accountability becomes important so that the leader can demonstrate what they are doing, even if progress is slow. That way the trust and accountability between DEI and leaders, and leaders and their employees can grow.

3.4 Understanding the aims and reasons

Are you and your allies, influencers and key stakeholders on the same page? I have found so many times that although my stakeholders have agreed on the 'why', they haven't agreed on the 'how'. This part of the puzzle can come down to cultural discrepancies or other forces; one such example being a generally different approach in the US and non-US market in the approach towards positive action. The US market is encouraged to use 'affirmative action' for underrepresented groups, whereas UK employers have to exercise extreme caution as this can breach legislative rules around illegal positive discrimination, and instead are encouraged to fix unjust processes and tailor the adverts and roles to match the skills and in some cases demographics of individuals.

In not so many words, the UK approach can see the US approach as a hollow solution or quick fix to the issue of representation as the matter of inclusion isn't addressed in this approach, whereas the US could see the UK approach as lacking urgency to redress the representation. It is critical that the 'why' is understood, and the 'why not' of what approaches are taken or not taken in the 'how' of execution is agreed by stakeholders.

3.5 Relevant data and insight

We often say that what we measure we can change, and there is truth in that statement. But we need to bridge that measurement … and change with a question. The question is: what is the data telling me, and can it be trusted?

For example, if my organisation is driven by data alone, I might never enact disability inclusion programmes. Disability representation, although being statistically large in the UK population, is rarely reported above 11 per cent in the workforce due to stigmas and other issues. Stigma around other characteristics may mean that the reality of the experience is not reflected in the data because of inequalities, trauma and biases which have stopped the disclosure from reaching us in the first place so that we can build a strategy based on that data.

So, ensure that you apply insight and interrogation to the data analysis. What is missing from the data, how does it compare to the national and industry averages, does the experience of people match the trends of the data? And a more fundamental question — how do you influence change, using data? If I am the only genderqueer person at your organisation, would you have a policy for me, or would I have to be 10 per cent of your population? Does data dictate how you prioritise or does it influence how you are informed?

3.6 Robust decision-making framework

Next we need to think about decision making. What are the frameworks we have in place to ensure that there is integrity and transparency at all levels of the DEI strategy formation and execution so that those who are involved, interested in, or benefitting from the strategy are able to understand why we are working on the aims we have chosen, using the tools we are using and comprehend how these decisions can be justified ethically and from a business perspective.

Some organisations use an EqIA framework, and others use a governance accountability mechanism. Take a moment and think about what framework you have in place to ensure transparency and integrity of the key stage-gate processes for decisions in your strategy formation and rollout? Where is accountability in your own creation and execution? Are your executive leaders rewarded based on company performance regardless of the cultural impact? How do you assess cultural impact, e.g. are you giving bonuses and STIPs (Short Term Incentives) based on representation, or inclusion, or something else? And is that really DEI or just one aspect of it?

3.7 Balanced action and communication

This is the 60:20:20 model we spoke about earlier, and an effective strategy will have an annual engagement plan linked to corporate touchpoints, external observance dates and opportunistic communication. The communication of action is critical in this part of the strategy, as the behaviour change of the organisation, or rather the people within it, can vary depending on what progress, or lack thereof, is perceived to be made in this space.

I recall an organisation with an anti-racism strategy being lambasted by its internal women's network and carers network that they didn't feel represented in the DEI approach (insert comment about whataboutism here). What the DEI team had failed to do was to explain how the actions taken to redress the inequities being faced by ethnic minorities in the UK, would actually end up benefitting all the demographics who represented a minority population in the organisation (e.g. revisiting the approach to UK Workforce Succession Planning).

The communication ratio of action to perception of action, and the packaging of initiatives are critical elements to consider as part of the components of an effective DEI strategy. When done effectively they can reduce the resistance or apathy, and instead bring clarity and alignment, which brings an increased energy to the direction of the strategic aims.

In this section we have examined the key elements of DEI theory essential to examine to be part of a meaningful and sustainable DEI Theory and Strategy. This includes understanding the business trajectory and how DEI adds value; the motivation to engage in the work; the groups to focus on upskilling; where impact can be most meaningful delivered; how activity can be structured to be perceived; and how challenge can be directed to add value.

SECTION 3: NOTHING TO EXCESS

SECTION 3
NOTHING TO EXCESS

Calls to action and imagining broad aims

Μηδὲν ἄγαν
(Nothing to Excess)

Chapter 1.
Caution and Reminders

One of the most powerful maxims that our genius Bias put together was 'nothing to excess'. It is a tenet of knowledge so universal it applies across all areas of our lives both within and outside of business. I find that this is perhaps one of the most helpful pieces of knowledge, and a reminder that we in the DEI space need more than some. We can find something that works in the DEI space and thereafter repeat it, copy and paste it and expect it to work for everyone. This is your reminder; one size does not fit all.

As driven practitioners ardently pursuing that social change and impact, we can find ourselves over-communicating, over-sharing, over-planning and generally over-extending ourselves to achieve our aims, sometimes lacking the understanding that these extremes we mistake for commitment unbalance us. Perhaps one of the areas we are most often challenged on, and rightly so, is an over-focus on particular demographic areas representing the whole of the DEI experience.

In this section we explore what devices, tools and approaches we have to deliver our change and how we need to balance these to be effective and relevant to the areas and communities we operate within and for.

I cannot tell you the number of DEI strategies and teams I have consulted or worked with who five and ten years into rolling out their strategy haven't even started to think about disability, or age, or sexual orientation. There is a difference between going deep on some issues to rectify injustices which affect us all, and consciously omitting the inclusion of broad demographics by a focus on a particular few.

This is a hard balance to get right, with any of these areas, but there are tools which can help us manage our focus and excesses, and these are quality data, reliable insight, standardised metrics, meaningful reporting and impact review & reflection.

In a profession which can be so innately linked with our personal experiences and individual purpose, we can find ourselves in a position where we can't see the wood for the trees in how far our impact is challenged. We are often so hungry for impact and impatient for action that we can find ourselves imbalanced when it comes to advocating for change for individuals, understanding the value to the business and choosing the best route and methods to achieve these actions.

This is where mindful reflection is essential to know what our blockers are and how we can be more effective. The exercises that we spoke through earlier on around the seasons and understanding your purpose and your position alignment are invaluable tools in helping you ensure that you are not driving change at the expense of your own or someone else's stability. We need to make sure that as practitioners we build and maintain our own space for that reflection. If we don't find time as practitioners to embed and maintain the space for reflection to understand our own motivation and challenges, we do a disservice to the communities which we seek to serve and may be less effective.

Some of the key challenges as well as some of the solutions which can help us address this balance is understanding how we utilise data, how we interpret it and how we report our progress. Although many of the challenges towards data interpretation are nuanced and require legal counsel to make them relevant and applicable to multiple jurisdictions, there are some general approaches which we can take that will be explored in the coming pages. This approach, an outline of how we can standardise and better use our data and insight, helps us balance where we measure our success and position our energies as practitioners.

1.1 Utilising data

We sometimes don't use data enough, and other times we use it to excess without verifying the validity or integrity of the information. One of the challenges we know we face with data is that in order to evidence that our approach is relevant, we need to have information often relating to representation of data to measure that. The issue with that is twofold. The first issue is that, of course, as we established, data lies. The second issue is that a lack of standardised data benchmarks across multiple industries, and sometimes even within single industries, represent a trial to us in properly understanding the challenges we are faced with and how to approach them.

Data integrity: Here's an example. One of my friends describes herself as working-class. She grew up with both of her parents in public sector jobs; one worked as a secretary, the other as a train driver. She never wanted for food or electricity when she was growing up. Another of my friends also describes herself as working-class. Her parents worked multiple jobs and couldn't afford always to pay energy, bills, or put food on the table. Both could be described as working-class by conventional standards designed in the 1930s, and later to describe the new social classes, but the experience and challenges which have been faced by them both are not representative when we have such broad groupings, designed decades ago, which don't represent the challenges or realities of today.

Data as a driver: Perhaps like me, you have been challenged by the sheer volume of data, which is collected and interpreted in the organisation, or perhaps such small amounts of data is collected that it's difficult to build in an evidence base for your approach beyond what you can demonstrate through visible, overt characteristics of diversity like ethnicity presented gender. Often, the lack of data or overwhelm of data can lead to the approach of starting with overt characteristics under the guise of efficiency; we focus on what we have evidence on. I have seen global companies go with this approach stating that we need to focus on ethnicity globally, and only then tailor their programs to focus on ethnicity within one particular country, as they quickly realise ethnicity is not a concept relevant to all of their local geographies to the same level.

Data credibility: You see, an evidence based approach needs to first ask the questions around the credibility and integrity of the data, and then, and only then, ask what the data is telling you. If an organisation wanted to get the 'biggest bang for its buck' it may focus its energies on demographics or characteristics which are most prevalent across the global geographies. It needs to understand what those demographics are globally and how that differed by region and geographic area. For instance, it may find in some areas that gender, sex, disability, and perhaps age and class are more relevant levers than focusing on LGBTQIA+ or religion. I won't speak for every company in what makes sense for them, but I encourage you as practitioners to challenge the direction of the organisational ambition globally and locally, and not to focus on particular 'global' demographics at the expense of local relevance. Is a decision in response to an expectation, or is it informed by credible data, integrity, and realistic insight, which will benefit a significant number of people across your organisation, geography, or global operating areas.

An informed and reflective practitioner will understand the challenges which data credibility and data integrity brings to the analysis of the data, and the subsequent identification of the DEI priorities. It's beholden on the practitioner to assess whether the data is representing the perceived reality of employees and whether that data represents a microcosm of society or is completely different to the challenges society faces. Then investigate why, before the priorities of that data become the focus for the organisational diversity and inclusion strategy.

1.2 Developing our insight

So, what do we really mean by insight? Well, to me insight is the difference between analysis and relevance. Insight gives us a true picture of the realities of what's happening; data gives us a static snapshot in time open to subjectivity.

Data, when it is interpreted effectively with appropriate benchmarks, relevance, control, mechanisms, and cleanliness routines can provide a real and compelling story for insight. But as we know, data has its limitations; it's only as good as the information which is entered in the first place.

This is where diversity and inclusion professionals have a special duty. So many of us will be able to resonate with the experience of being contacted by someone in the organisation whose experience differs entirely from what the organisation suggests is the norm for someone from that group. We may also know what it's like to be contacted by disabled colleagues or people from disadvantaged backgrounds, who are facing challenges which are not captured in the data of the business.

In the section, I won't go into too much detail about why we don't capture enough data about some of the concepts which affect the majority of the working population, such as disability or age. I will simply say that there seem to me to be two major challenges.

The first is that we segment the data too much to make it usable and find trends; for example, we may look at the difference between physical and mental disabilities and compare those results rather than look at the results between people who have and have not disclosed a disability.

Second is that there are long-standing issues, stigmas and trust gaps around what is done with the disclosed data. There are stories, even from my own life, where I can share how disclosure of a disability in an HR system has precipitated an occupational health referral, further compounding inequalities that I experience at work. Is it any wonder why there are lower disclosure rates for certain characteristics which can be hidden when systems, processes and behaviours are set up to actively include, but the end result actively excludes.

Next, I suggest, although we may have issues with the data which we currently collect as an organisation, we, as with any individual, interpreting data related to experience, are challenged with triaging what experience needs our attention most. Generally, in this space a utilitarian approach is employed where the scalability of our work in its ability to reach the greatest number of people is the precursor to action.

However, the maturity of our function in identifying areas of particular need through data and through insight is lacking. We may not even collect the data related to areas which need a focus most, or we may not analyse the data that way. For example, I may see in my data a great improvement overall in the experience of women or Black employees. However, I may not have built a reporting structure to look at the intersection of experience of Black Women, which may be particularly different to women. Overall, our maturity as a function in and our ability to focus on the greatest need as well as the highest impact is how we increase our relevance, both regionally and demographically.

1.3 Standardising global metrics

Too often I hear from individuals and companies that creating a companywide or group approach to diversity, equity and inclusion is impossible, because there are global data capture questions and options which can inform and evidence the approach. To me, this is a bit of a copout.

Yes, there are certain countries where we are not legally allowed to ask questions relating to diversity. And yes, there are some countries where legally we have a list of questions to ask relating to diversity. Those areas are known and a mature business will have that information to hand (if the business doesn't know that information, there are reams of material on the internet, which list those areas). Don't let fear of getting it wrong stop you from trying to get it right. Here is where you can examine your corporate risk appetite for the processing of DEI data as a whole, and it is an important conversation to have.

We cannot allow the complexity of reporting to stop us from capturing and analysing data. The challenge here is demographic relevance in a locally relevant market. For example, it would not be relevant for me to list the most dominant UK religions in the Indian market, just as it wouldn't be relevant to list the US ethnicity characteristics in the UK market, so how do we build a globally relevant diversity data capture system? I suggest through clearly separating out what data is captured at talent acquisition stage, and at on boarding stage.

At talent acquisition stage, we can ask general questions. We can ask a yes, no, and prefer not to say question related to any particular demographic and cross reference that response by the country in which they live. Simply put, I'm suggesting that instead of companies having a pre-set list of data, which they need candidates to choose from, they give the power to the candidate to self-disclose whether or not they identify as a minority. Here's an example:

Q: Do you identify as an ethnic minority in the country in which you live?

A: *Yes, no, prefer not to say.*

If we are able to capture data which is driven by employees own identification, we are one step closer with connecting to that employees lived experience. But there are challenges I hear you say. In some countries we have questions for talent acquisition which we need to ask, absolutely! And in those cases, there is nothing which stops us from pivoting and doing the process the other way around where we provide the drop-down of demographics they are legally obliged to choose from and ask this question, at the on boarding stage.

At the on boarding stage, we can ask candidates who have been asked and answered the broad question about self-identification 'yes / no /or prefer not to say', to provide us with more detail based on the country which they have stated they reside in. Most human resource information systems (HRISs) come preloaded with a drop-down of religions, ethnicities, or even disabilities relevant to the country where the employee has selected they live. If this is done at the on boarding stage, the data can be used during the course of the employee lifecycle as relevant. However, the data that we have collected around generally grouping individuals who self-identify at the talent acquisition stage, provides a valuable framework for inclusion practitioners, because no one person, practitioner or not, will have the knowledge of every country, region within the country and their individual demographic challenges with inclusion.

1.4 Meaningful reporting

We have spoken a little bit about how to build a compelling report with qualitative and quantitative data using milestones and KPIs, but we also need to remember how we tell the bigger picture of what we aren't reporting. As practitioners, we can navigate the tightrope between the existing expectations of the executive or the board and being drawn towards expanding our work for the betterment of broader demographics. Within our reporting, we must remember that representation and inclusion for the demographics that we have a focus on is appropriate, but we cannot forget to measure broader demographics, both at global and local level.

But where does it end I hear you ask? Do you want me to apply intersectional lenses, expand the demographics which we are focusing on and look at that globally and locally?! My simple answer is, yes. That's where we want to get to; that would be fantastic for individuals, mid managers, and leaders across businesses to have built into their KPIs and analysis of engagement. But I am a realist; we are not there yet and we won't be for some time. So we need to start with the demographics which are most relevant to your organisation, and the people within it.

When the reporting is underway, my suggestion is that the practitioners carefully take the time to add in the story of the demographics which have not been addressed yet and start to pepper-in the intersectional length of the demographics. For example, you may focus on disability and LGBTQIA+ status. Paint me a picture, what does a disabled LGBTQIA+ person's experience look like; are there a huge amount of those people in the organisation; does it matter if there's only one? Will their number impact your organisational importance in measuring? Are you doing something about it?

1.5 Review and reflection

Sometimes I can feel like I'm going at a billion miles an hour, trying to spin a thousand plates or run a hundred meetings, and sometimes I wish that there was a clone of me (though there are many other times I think that the world can only handle one of me!).

Although personal reflection and alignment to purpose is incredibly important, structure to the creation and execution of the strategy is paramount. The understanding of the theory behind DEI must inform that strategy. We also need individual practitioners to review their understanding of all of the above in a cycle. I see that cycle in six stages.

Hardy-Lenik DEI review and reflection cycle

1. The analysis of the 'as is' state.
2. Identification of the inclusion symptoms.
3. Identification of root causes of DEI challenges.
4. Building consensus, understanding and action.
5. Actioning the challenges through programming.
6. Measure and testing of impact.

The review must happen in stages and 1, 2, 3 and 6 are essential. To put that another way, four out of the six stages of a DEI approach involves reflection, review, and insight. In many cases we are 'doing' more than we are 'being', or 'executing' more than we are 'thinking'.

As effective practitioners, we need to hold ourselves accountable to this constant review, reflection and education of ourselves and our craft. We can do that through internal 360 reviews and performance appraisals from our colleagues within the business.

However, I believe the most impactful accountability mechanism I have to this constant review and learning practice comes from challenge from my industry, my peers, and by building networks of individuals who challenge me on what to action and when to action it, along with why I'm actioning it and why I am not actioning something else.

Accountability to your organisation drives action; accountability to your peers in industry drives reflection.

1.6 Telling the story in business terms

Business exists to make money; therefore DEI has to be able to articulate how it adds value to the bottom line of the business, whether that is in saving operating costs through effective talent management and engagement solutions, or through safe cognitive dissonance adding to innovation, or cultural intelligence opening up new markets and opportunities.

The tired narrative that diverse teams outperform homogenous teams is right — but, (and there is a very big BUT) — sometimes that is VERY wrong. Diversity alone doesn't guarantee diversity of thought. Diversity of thought doesn't guarantee innovation. In fact studies show that in some cases homogenous teams outperform diverse teams; there is a shared language, experience and approach from which to build a slick and effective way of working that logic tracks. So why do we say diverse teams are more effective?

Well, it is more nuanced than just being diverse. Diverse teams which are culturally intelligent outperform homogenous teams. Teams which enable cognitive dissonance free from repercussion outperform homogenous teams.

The focus shifts from representation to behaviours and actions of diverse representation. This is such a tiny nuance with humongous implications. Often we see businesses focused on the representation whilst cultural intelligence plays second fiddle or isn't even acknowledged as the secret sauce to unlock that diversity of experience.

If we move our approach beyond activism, i.e. doing DEI because we want to fix the immediate issues, and beyond representation alone, then we can start to approach a meaningful way to unlock innovation, collaboration and sustained engagement, which has a tangible impact to the bottom line of the business.

How do we do that? You will have seen this as a common theme throughout these pages, that in order to balance a meaningful and sustainable DEI approach which adds value to the business we need to address:

- The immediate inclusion issues
- The locally relevant representation gaps
- The systemic root causes of inequalities

I suggest in order for the important work which we have begun to increase representation, and inclusion to be sustained and continually invested in, we need to develop the behaviours, processes and systems which support cognitive dissonance free from repercussion as a basic approach and build upon that to reward healthy challenge and diversity of perspective being shared.

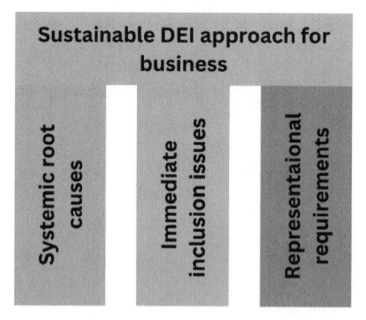

Hardy-Lenik sustainable DEI change areas

In this section we touched upon how businesses can unlock impact and return on DEI investment to the bottom line by ensuring that the systems, processes and behaviours to support cognitive dissonance free from repercussion are in place and advance the work of representational diversity and reinforce inclusive practices and the addressing of these engagement and inclusion needs.

If an organisation fails to focus on all three of these elements, the long term sustainability of their DEI function could be called into question. The value which the function has to help the business unlock the impact of people (the greatest asset of any business), to achieving its corporate aims, regardless of whether that is financial growth, stability or non-financial performance related to a non-profit sector is huge. DEI is the differentiating factor in people engagement, product and service development and innovation.

Ultimately DEI is the differentiating factor for business sustainability. Academics may link this more to social engineering or business psychology, and there is some more work to be done in this space to unpack the psychology of inclusion in business and how this narrative is explained in the business cases beyond representation.

SECTION 4: CALLS TO ACTION

SECTION 4
CALLS TO ACTION

Calls to action and imagining broad aims

There are some distinct areas which we as practitioners can focus on to meaningfully shift the dial on integrating inclusion into our businesses. I suggest that there are several key areas which we need, as practitioners, to agree upon as a shared narrative. The calls to action are;

1. Balancing Inclusion & Representation activity

2. Agreeing what skills/experiences required to be a practitioner

3. Cleansing and building our data credibility

4. Personal reflection

5. Telling the business story

Indeed, these calls to action which I repeat are a theme throughout the book, and some of the suggested approach is in how we can go about combating the challenges to the sustainability of the DEI function. These issues have been alluded to, but this is not a task for one person alone, or even a group of twenty. I suggest this requires a cumulative action to create sustainability and advocate a movement in this space. Let's name the issues as calls to action below.

Chapter 1.
Calls to Action

Calls to action

1.1 Balancing inclusion and representation activity

We've discussed many times about the need to meaningfully understand representation and the inclusion scores of employees. We must come to a point within our industry where we no longer except representational diversity to be driving all of the conversation and targets. Representational diversity in all its forms is incredibly important; it is, however only half of the story. After all, what is inclusion if it doesn't represent diverse groups of people, and what's the purpose of representation if people don't feel included. We need to get better at pushing back the expectation that diversity, inclusion, equity and belonging is about a numbers game to do with whose bums are on seats and challenging the brand-imagery gains from representational diversity as the end-goal for some organisations who do this work a disservice.

1.2. Agreeing what skills/experiences are required to be a practitioner

Goodwill alone is not enough to sustain someone operating as a successful practitioner. In this space we need to agree on what are the core concepts, experiences, and skills essential to make the change we are looking to achieve in this work. We also need to name the issues in collaboration and conversation to provide clarity to people within our own industry, and beyond. This will help us sustain how to balance representation and experience as part of a criteria for being in a diversity, equity and inclusion role. As we have outlined, our experiences give us access to knowledge and issues that can help us be better practitioners, but the skill in the way we channel those experiences requires alignment and consideration across the profession, so that we are ensuring true representational diversity within the space, and that the skills that are being hired to lead this work are done so in a sustainable way.

1.3 Cleansing and building our data credibility

We need to have better data standards, better data alignment, and more relevant reporting options. We know that some of our data groupings are relevant to broad groups of people, we know that global approaches to collecting data can present challenges, and we know that organisations can be slow to the intersectionality of the data it collects. As a profession, we need to define where global metrics can be aligned, perhaps, with a start in industry, and where our regional and geographic metrics can be aligned to greatest effect.

1.4 Personal reflection

In order to be good leaders and wise practitioners, we need to make the time to know when we are off centre from what makes us tick.

We need to know when to stand back from pursuing a particular course of action, when we need to let it go beyond our control, what we need to endure and how we need to plan more effectively. To be good leaders and wise leaders, it goes beyond knowledge and subject matter expertise; a good leader in this space will take the time to analyse themselves, the origin of their knowledge, the credibility of that knowledge, and the alignment to their personal purpose, direction, and position. Then, the theory and the execution will have a sustainable build for years to come.

So much of the DEI space requires us to have conversations about authenticity, and promote authenticity as a key desired outcome, which comes from a sense of belonging and inclusion. I suggest that understanding the source of our knowledge, construct, overthinking, and the patterns of our actions, enables us to employ a more authentic approach in our own leadership of diversity, equity and inclusion. The need for cognisant, sometimes methodical, and on occasion painfully slow self-reflection, will be a key enabler to help us sustain our momentum, rather than just actioning our pre-determined plans.

1.5. Telling the business story in commercial language

Have you ever heard of a business firing or making redundant a function which enables a significant production of revenue? There are of course exceptions, but we need to make it hard for companies to get rid of our functions We can do this by aligning our language to the business language of profit or purpose (commercial viability of DEI), and talking about the change we steward beyond the soft change initiatives of a training event here and an ERG there. We need to help businesses understand the bottom line impact, the 'hard impact' to the business. This impact will vary depending on the organisation, though will likely cover the costs of engagement and workforce management, the opportunity for innovation and reduced rework cycles or greater product/service relevance, and increased brand identity leading to investment and reduced risk from external reporting scrutiny.

Chapter 2.
Some Broad Aims

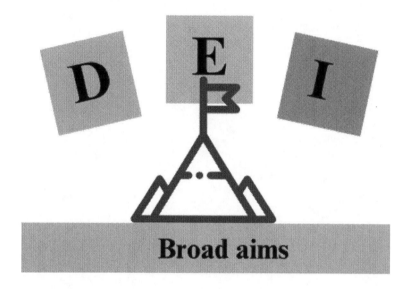

As one individual, I don't have a complete answer to how we collectively go about taking this set of actions forward. Of course there are isolated areas where, for instance, I could push forward collaboration in partnership in my own network, but that reach is limited as it will be for any individual. However, if all of us, within our respective networks, advocate for these changes, or these calls to action from a personal and professional perspective, we may as a group find an ability to achieve a more targeted impact on our business areas than we have seen in years.

The Benefits We Could See if
We Focus on These Actions

If we managed to achieve a level of business integration from addressing these calls to action, I believe the results would be profound, with an impact upon:

1. *The sustainability of the DEI function (resource).*
2. *Empathic dispersed leadership.*
3. *Increased equitable processes.*
4. *Inclusive skills.*
5. *Increased engagement & innovation.*
6. *Community impact.*

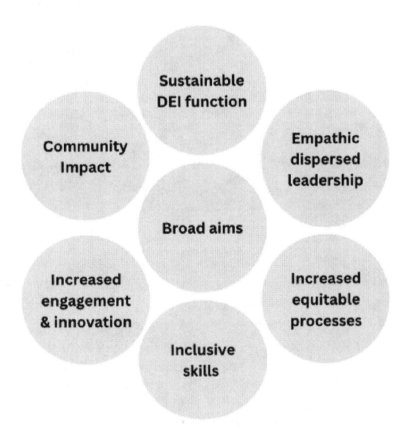

2.1 The sustainability of the DEI function

Once the function has been able to prove its value to the organisation, the continued resource and access for its longevity can be more easily assured.

Additionally, once the skills, experiences, and overall competencies I've been outlining for the continued development and sustainability of the profession have been agreed in some format and adopted by multiple organisations to understand and apply those competencies, there is likely a greater chance of practitioners being set up to succeed. Practitioners will be hired with the required skill sets to execute the role required of them, and this creates a clearer career pathway for aspirational, DEI change-makers. I also suggest that the solid understanding of the theory outlined in the early sections of this book, as well as the robust adherence to the creation, execution and review of that strategy will enable a more sustainable function for years to come, with greater transparency, and understanding of the approach, available to colleagues, allies, and advocates.

2.2 Empathic dispersed leadership

As our approach towards balancing inclusion and representation develops, my experience has shown that inclusion lessons are sometimes learned by those in positions of influence, whether that influence comes from the legitimate power of being a senior leader, or whether it's through the referent power of being a subject matter expert in the organisation, or a respected voice in a particular function, region or community. As we sustain the function and practice of diversity, equity and inclusion, through our sound application of theory and our development and stewardship of the conversation relating to the core tenets of humanity, we engage in the paradox of DEI, which we mentioned earlier; a concept which requires simplification of the core message of our work, as well as a deep level understanding and application of the concept and levers to supercharge it.

As the return on investment to the function is beginning in places to be fully realised, alongside greater understanding on what meaningful reporting looks like being understood by the leadership of an organisation, we may find that the practitioner will have to spend less time coaching leadership to recognise the distinct skills required to do the role. They could then focus more of their energy onto building a collaborative and convening narrative and collation of changemakers where leaders (however leadership is defined), are encouraged, rewarded and guided on how to develop increasingly compassionate, people-centred, and ultimately empathic approaches to their work. This would then be overlaid with our continued work on representational diversity. I believe it is reasonable to hope that should the function of DEI be properly integrated into a business, there is greater room for empathic dispersed leadership across multiple geographies and functions.

2.3 Increased equitable processes

We can identify root cause issues, address inequalities, and build equity rebalancing plans. It's not unreasonable to assume that if we were to pay close attention to the behaviours, systems and processes which comprise the organisation's ability as a whole to affect the experience of an employee, and actively balance our work between representation, inclusion and identifying the root causes of those inequalities, then the work of representation and engagement will likely force practitioners to delve into the barriers affecting root cause issues beyond engagement and representation. Practitioners will play a part in building a societal element of equity where appropriate, once the root causes of equality have been identified and challenged.

This could range from a review of a policy through to some kind of targeted action of the demographic group. It is also worth noting that in some countries where positive action or affirmative action is encouraged, or legally permitted, the path towards securing an equitable approach can be achieved more easily from a regulatory perspective. I would, though, encourage practitioners in these regions to consider whether fast track equity programs fix those systemic issues or just put a rosier complexion on the existing issues.

2.4 Inclusive skills

In earlier pages we discussed the balance between the need to focus on behaviours, systems and processes, and infrastructure. We demonstrated how all of those components are inherently interlinked when it comes to behaviour, change, and an integrated DEI approach, which truly has the ability to transform the business and will be in a unique position to build and sustain what inclusive skills looks like within the organisation.

Inclusive skills can begin manifesting within the different levels of collaboration, consultation and co-production and can be nurtured into allyship and leadership of inclusive skills through an intentional and targeted focus of which individuals or groups of individuals you're seeking to move from a particular competence range to another; for example, from conscious incompetence all the way through to conscious competence and unconscious competence.

The continued development of the inclusive skillset is a key differentiator in what good leadership looks like, and an increasingly important skillset to the upcoming new generation of workers. In the last few years, we have seen an increased appetite for emotional intelligence (EQ) and cultural intelligence (CQ) across multiple organisations, including organisations which only have a national presence, demonstrating to me that there is a development in people's understanding of the need for knowledge, and awareness of self, as one of the foundations towards building an inclusive skillset.

2.5 Increased engagement and innovation

When you treat people correctly, when they feel safe to challenge and contribute, and when they know there will be a fair process of reward and remuneration, they want to do more; that's the theory. Another way to express this is also known as an employer's access to discretionary motivation. I don't tend to use those more complex academic words; sometimes I feel that hiding behind the complexities of those words can make it a little difficult to understand the meaning. But I think this is one of the simplest concepts, which we haven't yet got right because we have only started to scratch the surface.

So much of our work has been focused on trying to change culture through silos, behavioural and incidental structural reforms to organisations rather than a holistic root cause identification alongside representational diversity and immediate inclusion issues being balanced in the approach to reflect the needs of the organisation. I know that I would be far more likely to engage if I knew it was safe to make a mistake; I know I would work harder if I had a greater sense of job security and fair recognition; and I know I would be challenged more if different characteristic groups expressed cognitive dissonance around me. These are just isolated examples, from one individual, throughout this book. We've had a few examples of the real bottom-line impact which innovation and engagement can have on the business or the organisation's success and can be the differentiator between success and sustainability, or failure of an organisation.

2.6 Community impact

Socially conscious organisations will recognise that although there are root causes in the business hindering equity and inclusion, there also exist complex societal issues, steeped in history. Many global organisations have now signed up to the

UN Global Compact and align their ESG credentials according to the UN Sustainable Development Goals (SDGs), which demonstrates their intent in the Environmental, Social and Governance (ESG) aspects of their footprint. When organisations are intentional about aligning their organisational priorities with their social impact credentials, they can not only benefit from the partnership in collaboration, not to mention future possibility of markets being opened up, but they also contribute to the erasure of barriers through affording opportunities where investment has historically not been forthcoming.

Although, we must remember as practitioners that we might wear, several hats — an internal business hat as a DEI business leader or an external hat, as a rights and equity advocate — this is one of those happy times where those two identities are welcomed to intersect and I believe we, as practitioners, have a great contribution to make to the developing ESG space as it develops over the coming years.

A wonderful quotation from the 1980s BBC series *Yes Prime Minister* goes 'A cynic, is what an optimist calls a realist', and although I do truly believe that I am being realistic when I say that I believe that this work will outlast my lifetime by a significant margin, I live in hope of being proven a cynic.

My last few words remain to say 'thank you', to you for reading this and giving this small collection of words your kind attention and reflection, to recognise and applaud the celebrated and the uncelebrated practitioners, allies and advocates in this space, to wish you peace and serenity and finally to encourage you to go out and be something unapologetic, loud and totally you.

This work won't always be easy, and so the parting wisdom I leave you with are two quotations which have shaped my life; 'try and be the person you needed when you were younger' and 'remember that life starts at the end of your comfort zone'.

About the Author

Tim (T) has over a decade of experience affecting diversity, equity and inclusion change in a variety of industries across the corporate and third sectors.

Tim has been recognised though various accolades as a global leader of diversity, equity and inclusion. They have served upon multiple boards, committees, networks and projects, including cross industry networks for diversity practitioners and projects which defined precedent setting DEI theory.

They have chaired work within multiple sectors to advance human rights, inclusion and ESG ranging from the sports industry, medicine and charities and a wide range of private sector organisations.

Tim chaired an Industry Group which launched the world's first comprehensive score to improve corporate and cross-industry evidence based approaches to advance diversity and inclusion.

Tim uses their own experiences of a gay, disabled, genderqueer, proud father and survivor to tell their own story, and attempt to simplify the complex world of DEI, by fostering human connection, celebrating kindness and nurturing respect, which is, the key tenets of humanity and inclusion.

Tim is a Fellow of the Society of Leadership Fellows at St George's House, Windsor Castle and a Fellow of the Royal Society of Arts, Manufacturing and Commerce.

Follow Tim Hardy-Lenik, BA. Hons Winc, CIPD, FRSA
linkedin.com/in/timhardy1/

BUSINESS
BOOKS

Business Books

Business Books publishes practical guides
and insightful non-fiction for beginners and professionals.
Covering aspects from management skills, leadership and
organizational change to positive work environments, career
coaching and self-care for managers, our books are a valuable
addition to those working in the world of business.

Recent bestsellers from Business Books are:

From 50 to 500
Jonathan Dapra, Richard Dapra and Jonas Akerman
An engaging and innovative small business leadership
framework guaranteed to strengthen a
leader's effectiveness to drive company growth and results.
Paperback: 978-1-78904-743-1 ebook: 978-1-78904-744-8

Be Visionary
Marty Strong
Be Visionary: Strategic Leadership in the Age of Optimization
Demonstrates to existing and aspiring
leaders the positive impact of applying visionary creativity
and decisiveness to achieve spectacular
long-range results while balancing the day-to-day.
Paperback: 978-1-78535-432-8 ebook: 978-1-78535-433-5

Finding Sustainability
Trent A. Romer
Journey to eight states, three national parks and three
countries to experience the life-changing
education that led Trent A. Romer to find sustainability for his
plastic-bag manufacturing business and himself.
Paperback: 978-1-78904-601-4 ebook: 978-1-78904-602-1

Inner Brilliance, Outer Shine
Estelle Read
Optimise your success, performance, productivity and
well-being to lead your best business life.
Paperback: 978-1-78904-803-2 ebook: 978-1-78904-804-9

Tomorrow's Jobs Today
Rafael Moscatel and Abby Jane Moscatel
Discover leadership secrets and technology strategies being
pioneered by today's most innovative
business executives and renowned brands across the globe.
Paperback: 978-1-78904-561-1 ebook: 978-1-78904-562-8

Secrets to Successful Property Investment
Deb Durbin
Your complete guide to building a property portfolio.
Paperback: 978-1-78904-818-6 ebook: 978-1-78904-819-3

The Effective Presenter
Ryan Warriner
The playbook to professional presentation success!
Paperback: 978-1-78904-795-0 ebook: 978-1-78904-796-7

The Beginner's Guide to Managing
Mikil Taylor
A how-to guide for first-time managers adjusting to their new
leadership roles.
Paperback: 978-1-78904-583-3 ebook: 978-1-78904-584-0

Forward
Elizabeth Moran
A practical playbook for leaders to guide their teams through
their organization's next big change.
Paperback: 978-1-78279-289-5 ebook: 978-1-78279-291-8

Readers of ebooks can buy or view any of these bestsellers by clicking on the live link in the title. Most titles are published in paperback and as an ebook. Paperbacks are available in traditional bookshops. Both print and ebook formats are available online.
Find more titles and sign up to our readers' newsletter at http://www.jhpbusiness-books.com/
Follow us on Facebook Read to Succeed with John Hunt Publishing